When Life Becomes a Maze

Discovering Christ's Resources for Times of Confusion

When Life Becomes a Maze

Discovering Christ's Resources for Times of Confusion

David R. Mains

"What to Do"
Chapter Endings by Laurie Mains

Destiny Image Publishers, Inc.®
P.O. Box 310
Shippensburg, PA 17257-0310

"Speaking to the Purposes of God
for this Generation
and for the Generations to Come"

ISBN 1-879050-77-3

For Worldwide Distribution
Printed in the U.S.A.

First Printing: 1995   Second Printing: 1995

Destiny Image books are available through many distributors outside the United States.

Inside the U.S., call toll free to order:
1-800-722-6774

Dedicated to K.P. Yohannan,
"A friend who sticks closer than a brother."
Without his help
the 1996 50-Day Spiritual Adventure
would not have taken place.

Contents

Introduction

How relieved I felt to put the eight chapters of this book behind me! A horrendous year had provided more than enough personal experiences to authentically illustrate the biblical principles under consideration. Hope prompted me to think that finishing the manuscript also meant this pain-filled chapter of my life was completed. Praise the Lord!

All that remained was to write this introduction.

I'll do it after my long overdue week of vacation, I told myself. *In a short while the promised foundation grants will begin: first $250,000, then another $200,000, and finally $500,000.* With a ministry budget around five million dollars a year, those matching grants would be a huge boost in paying the up-front costs of underwriting the 1996 50-Day Spiritual Adventure: "What to Do When You Don't Know What to Do: Trusting Christ When Life Gets Confusing." I felt so grateful to God for the soon-to-come funds, and I felt grateful to our donors who had been extremely generous in their response to this matching grant challenge.

I returned to work rested from the week away and eager to begin again. It was eight o'clock on Monday morning when I sat at my desk and the phone rang. It was our board chairperson asking if I had seen the lead article in *The Wall Street Journal*. I hadn't, so he informed me that the Foundation for New Era Philanthropy was on the brink of bankruptcy. Our grants were in jeopardy, and he thought I should check things out.

By five o'clock that afternoon the bankruptcy announcement was official, and all of a sudden my world was in chaos again. Instead of being financially stabilized, The Chapel Ministries had once more plunged into the middle of a maze. Intense feelings of anxiety returned. I dreaded the embarrassment of talking with my staff about this disastrous turn of events. Were their jobs secure? Could we possibly continue? I was reluctant to call the contributors who had given toward this matching grant, and inform them that their money had been lost.

That's exactly the new muddle I'm working my way through as I write this Introduction to meet my publisher's print deadline.

Consequently, I've gone back and reread the chapters that follow. Do I still believe what I wrote? Yes. But circumstances are forcing me to affirm the value of these principles more by faith than by sight. If a book's reality factor is important, then let it be known that the following pages are written not only for others, but also for myself.

Every year when a 50-Day Spiritual Adventure is put together, we discover that our planning forums often take on prophetic overtones. Materials must be prepared that will be appropriate for the Church long after the time they were first conceived. Apparently this theme of "trusting Christ when life gets confusing" is one that God feels needs to be examined throughout the ranks of churchgoers. I sense that our Lord knows large numbers of people who will benefit from advice about "what to do when you don't know what to do!"

I have lived a sheltered and protected life compared to others. The pain that my spiritual brothers and sisters have experienced in many places of the world has not been my experience. Hunger, persecution, and many kinds of loss have not been my lot. *But* I am learning more about confusion and suffering. My prayer is that these lessons will continue to prove valuable for myself, my family, and my staff, as well as for those who apply the biblical principles in this book for many days to come.

David R. Mains

Chapter 1

God Will Make a Way

Last autumn I took my two-year-old granddaughter to a reconstructed farm in the nearby Chicago suburbs. A simple maze had been put together for children out of bales of hay, and little Caitlyn loved running through the corridors and jumping off the walls. In Lancaster County, Pennsylvania, I've been told, large mazes are cut into the midst of some of the corn fields. Many times landscapers planted a labyrinth of boxwood or yew hedges in the middle of formal English gardens.

Mazes come in different forms; some are more challenging than others, some less so. To get into the world of more *difficult* mazes, puzzle-solvers tackle computer games. For most of us, however, just living life for a while is enough to experience our share of complexities. Sooner or later, we reach a point where there seems to be no exit or entrance; no escape from some terrible, pain-filled dead end.

I've been trying to recall where I was emotionally about a year ago. That's when I found myself in a seemingly impossible maze that I'm still trying to master. It started with a series of negative articles by "watchdogs of the faith" who questioned the authenticity of my ministry. The accusations first focused on my wife Karen's writing. She's had 20 or more books published with evangelical publishing houses—and some have been national prize-winners. Because of her high reputation, the criticism that she was a proponent of New Age thinking seemed unbelievable. But indeed, that's what a couple of critics were suggesting.

Suddenly, our office phones were ringing and ringing with inquiries from concerned pastors, Christian radio station managers, and long-time supporters. Next, our accusers questioned not only Karen, but also me. By quoting out of context, by imposing meanings never intended, they raised issue with broadcast topics or articles that I had written as many as ten years before. We suddenly felt like we were before a modern Inquisition tribunal.

Not knowing all that much about New Age thinking, I was incredulous and predicted that the storm would soon blow over. I couldn't have been more wrong.

In another month I was literally terrified over what was occurring. Stations on which "The Chapel of the Air" had broadcast for decades were dropping the program. The original negative articles were being quoted by others who stretched the ludicrous statements even more; donations fell off drastically; ministering peers were requesting answers to their long letters of inquiry that would have required a full-time research team to adequately satisfy. I was like the proverbial frightened mouse that not only didn't know how to get out of this maze, but also kept bumping into the electric shock mechanism no matter which way it fled. Eventually our radio debt was so large that we were forced to close the doors of the broadcast, despite its past history of some 55 years of ministry.

What do you do when you don't know what to do?

To be honest, I'm not capable of answering that for you from the perspective of someone who has already worked his way through his entanglements. I'm getting closer to the end of this puzzle, and I'm really anxious to break out into open ground—even though I may find myself in totally new territory. But I'm not at the end yet.

So what I'm sharing are the spiritual lessons I learned while still in the maze. I can tell you what's working for me and what's not. I apologize if my thoughts aren't as finished as I would like; in truth, I've never addressed these specific matters before. Still—my writing is relevant to where I am. That I can guarantee.

Not everyone will identify with the immediate need of mastering a given maze. But almost all of us know a family member or well-loved friend who is having to endure a seemingly hopeless situation. Sooner or later, everyone faces one of life's mazes.

As a student, for example, you may be facing a financial labyrinth. A scholarship didn't come through, parents weren't able to help as much as they would like, and now paying bills is a more immediate priority than getting good grades. At best, this semester will end with deep debt. Maybe you're even training for a ministry position or a helping profession that doesn't promise too much in future financial returns.

Thinking about graduate school is not realistic, but in order to achieve long-range professional plans, not going to graduate school isn't realistic either. Changing majors is a possibility, but that's already happened twice. Perhaps seeing a doctor about the burning in your stomach is important, but maybe it's just as well you don't know what's causing the pain. It can't just be stress, can it?

On top of that, the student world is filled with romantic dead ends. Someone loves someone who is in love with someone else. On top of even all this, how in the world does one discern the mind of the Lord—a maze of another incredibly perplexing kind?

Student culture today is a microcosm of perplexities. Seniors graduate and often haven't the faintest idea what they should do—except maybe move back home with mom and dad and look for a job in the hometown they vowed they would never live in again.

Are these just words? Every sub-culture has an inherent set of imponderables. The doctor has health care mazes and malpractice insurance predicaments. Lawyers have one of the highest rates of depression. Housewives must cope with troublesome marriages, troubled adolescents, and the rise of the troubling feminist agenda.

Mazes are sooner or later a part of everyday life.

These impossible-to-solve puzzles can be found in all countries of the world. Maybe as a young man in India your conversion came about because of the efforts of Western missionaries. But your early dependance on them was brought to a screeching halt when your country closed its doors to foreigners with beliefs incompatible with Hinduism. Suddenly it seemed all the spiritual help you needed was gone and you felt abandoned by the very God who made Himself known to you in such a personal way. The job of evangelism within your own country was immense, but you were young and inexperienced and had only limited resources. What were you supposed to do when you didn't know what to do?

In stories, a maze can trap anyone unexpectedly. Remember the innocent passengers in the movie *Speed*? They're on this bus that has exceeded 50 miles per hour, and now if the speed drops below that mark, a hidden bombing mechanism will explode. Suddenly they're hostage to some lunatic saboteur's reckless revenge. Real life can be a lot like those crazy stories. As the head of an organization, I have to make sure that the Chapel doesn't explode, that nobody gets hurt, and that the "bomb" is somehow diffused. How did I ever get into this situation?

One of the things I've learned this past horrific year is that lots of people are riding such buses! Little devotional talks from ministers or well-meaning Christians won't cut it for them. Platitudes are useless to those lost in a real-life labyrinth. I'm grateful to the Lord for the opportunity to understand on a deep level what many are experiencing. For most, unlike the ending of *Speed*, there's not even the promise of a romance with the adorable Sandra Bullock or the handsome Keanu Reeves!

For you who are lost in a pain-filled predicament, let me welcome you to the "In the Maze Club." Would you believe membership goes all the way back to Bible times? The Book of Genesis tells about Joseph, a young man who looked like he had it made. His father's favorite son, Joseph had also received unusual God-given prophetic promises through his dreams.

Then, while off looking for his jealous brothers, Joseph was quickly and unexpectedly transported as a captive to his special land of confusion. But losing his way didn't mean he lost his contact with

God. It was his strong belief that God was with him that eventually brought Joseph to his place of prominence in Egypt. Words spoken much later to his humble and repentant brothers have become a hallmark for all who suffer from the evil actions of others: "So then, it was not you who sent me here, but God.... You intended to harm me, but God intended it for good to accomplish what is now being done, the saving of many lives" (Gen. 45:8; 50:20).

This same conviction was expressed by David (again as a young man). If Samuel spoke for God and anointed David as king, why was David having to play the Harrison Ford role of *The Fugitive*? Confused by what was happening, in Psalm 27 David nevertheless wrote in verses 2 and 3, then 13:

> *When evil men advance against me to devour my flesh, when my enemies and my foes attack me, they will stumble and fall. Though an army besiege me, my heart will not fear; though war break out against me, even then will I be confident. ... I am still confident of this: I will see the goodness of the Lord in the land of the living.*

In other words, "With God's help I'll make it through this maze."

Those of us not yet free of the confusion can't help but admire such spiritual pluck. "I am still confident of this: I will see the goodness of the Lord in the land of the living." Now, that's faith!

In essence, these spiritual forebears remind us of a key truth that those of us in the middle of our puzzles need to put to use: *When life is confusing, choose to believe the Lord will make a way for you through the maze.*

The opposite would be to assume that God is really not all that interested in our situation.

Or that He doesn't have time to get involved in our petty needs.

Or that He wants us to work things through totally on our own.

Or that these passages of Scripture really aren't all that applicable to dilemmas like being maxed out on both our Visa and MasterCard with no way of stopping additional bills from coming.

Or that "my way is hidden from the Lord; my cause is disregarded by my God" (Is. 40:27b).

Wait! writes the prophet in verses 30 and 31. Let me contemporize a little:

Even youths grow tired and weary running down passageways that appear promising but in reality are dead ends, *and young men* and women *stumble and fall* and bump into walls and hedges and cornstalks and hay bales; *but those who hope in the Lord will renew their strength. They will soar on wings like eagles; they will run and not grow weary, they will walk and not be faint.*

In the New Testament, the same basic truth is proclaimed in Romans 8: When life is confusing, choose to believe that Christ will make a way for you through the maze!

And we know that in all things God works for the good of those who love Him, who have been called according to His purpose. ...If God is for us, who can be against us? He who did not spare His own Son...how will He not also, along with Him, graciously give us all things?... For I am convinced that neither death nor life, neither angels nor demons, neither the present nor the future...nor anything else in all creation—including bills, or broken relationships, or unfulfilled promises, or misunderstandings, or a need for counselling, or a spiritual burden for a land like India that's far bigger than what most people pray about, or mazes of any kind... (Romans 8:28,31-32,38-39).

I know I'm adding words. But the text reads, "nor *anything else in all creation*, will be able to separate us from the love of God that is in Christ Jesus our Lord." I was just listing a few of the "anything elses" that can't separate us from God.

It is when life is most confusing that we have the opportunity to test these truths. Do we believe them or not?

In fact, our words give away where our convictions lie. We should take note of our words. We need to listen closely to what we are saying. Our remarks give us clues about what we really believe. In the maze, do we tell others, "I'll never get through this. I know I won't!" Do we fret, "I don't think I'm going to make it. There's no way out of this dilemma."

Or do we speak what Scripture teaches? "I believe God is working in a marvelous way in my behalf. What he's doing just hasn't been revealed yet. But it's going to be like Joseph's story all over again. I'm trusting the Lord for that!"

"How are you doing, David Mains?" someone asks. "Are you practicing what you preach?"

"Well, I'm going through a hard time," I respond, "but I'm growing spiritually. And you know what? In this great test of my faith, I'm choosing to believe that God is working to pull off something wonderful."

Hebrews 11 is the listing of the Old Testament heroes of the faith (both men and women). Here's verse 6: "And without faith it is impossible to please God, because anyone who comes to Him must believe that He exists and that He rewards those who earnestly seek Him."

Hey! Am I making it all too simple in light of the terrible problems you may be facing? If so, allow me to talk to myself.

"David, your radio ministry (with a history of 55 years) had to shut down. That was painful, especially since the program was begun by your uncle. It was like you were the person who sold the family farm. But the new daily television ministry is doing well. With only a year and a half on air, 'You Need to Know' has already received the Television Program of the Year Award from the National Religious Broadcasters. Is that the direction God is pointing out to you? It was scary to quit radio. You didn't want to make a wrong decision. Will you believe that God is going before you, walking you through the various stages of this maze? And will you thank Him for His guidance, or will you grouse, complain, and malign the Lord as though He wasn't caring for you the way He should?"

Well, I, David Mains, am determined to be an "I believe" person. I'm going to keep repeating the words of faith. I'm confident that I'll see the goodness of the Lord in the land of the living. That's what I'm going to do. So I'm encouraging all who read these words to be "I believe" people right along with me.

Too many times in Christian circles we say, "This is never going to work out. Things are a mess. There's no solution." Those are death words; they imply that God isn't working all things together for good for those who love Him and are called according to His purpose.

I like what I would call an "I believe" sequence in the recent adaptation of the movie *Miracle on 34th Street*. Did you see it over the Christmas season? (If you don't mind, I'll use a number of film illustrations in this book. With the coming of television I find church people identify more quickly with these stories than with illustrations from books.) This particular movie questions whether this old fellow, played by Richard Attenborough, could really be Santa Claus. The judge knows he's not, but he has a dilemma. If in his courtroom he rules the old man isn't St. Nick, he risks destroying the belief in Santa that all the kids in New York City hold. That's a tough position to be in, especially when the story of the trial is in all the newspapers. Then the city rallies. All across the metropolitan area adults begin putting up signs saying, "I believe." It's written in the graffiti; it's on the sides of the buses; even store windows display "I believe" cards. The hard hat workers repeat the words, and so do the symphony orchestra members. Everybody's saying the same thing: "I believe." Thus the growing momentum of belief carries the day.

But I fear we've lost the "I believe" momentum when it comes to the truth of the universe. Maybe people of the Church don't believe anymore like they used to. As soon as we hit a big bump, we suddenly stop believing. Are we still saying the "I believe" statements in the church board meetings, in the choir rehearsals, the Sunday school lessons, the missions fundraisers, the hospital visitations, and the finance department emergencies?

I fear we're too often like the disciples in the final days of Christ's earthly life. Those were confusing and troubling times for His Twelve. In John 14, Thomas says in essence, "We're lost. We don't even know where You're going, Lord, so how can we know the way?" That's maze talk!

Christ responds, "I am the way. And on top of that, I'm going to ask the Father to give you another besides Myself to counsel you and to be with you forever. He'll teach you *all things*." Certainly that includes negotiating life's mazes.

The first principle I must learn in order to successfully negotiate life's mazes, then, is this: It's important to determine to be an "I believe" person.

Learn to tell yourself, "I have no doubt that Christ will make a way for me through this present confusion. Therefore my ears will consistently hear my mouth affirming that truth, until unbelief statements are all but eliminated. Though I'm not yet sure how, I have every confidence that my Lord is at work pulling off something good, creative, and surprising for me. I don't want to mess that up by allowing my own disbelief to rob me of that good and surprising future. I am determined to be known by God as an 'I believe' person."

Are you out of the maze yet? Probably not. Am I? No. But that doesn't mean we can't be "I believe" people!

Am I frustrated rewalking some of the paths of this maze over and over again? Not really. It's just a matter of time, for I'm learning to walk them by faith, believing that God is with me. The Master of all mazes will free me. Before long the open fields and an unblocked horizon will greet me.

Making "I believe" statements, choosing to believe in God's great provisions, builds my confidence in His amazing maze-solving skills. That's my first step in negotiating life's labyrinths.

What to Do

Here are some suggestions to help you live out what you've learned in this chapter.

1. Learn from everyday objects. You sit in a chair and it holds your weight. You turn a key and your car starts. You flick a switch and the light turns on. If it's so easy to believe that a fax machine can transmit a dozen pages halfway across the country, why is it so difficult to believe that God can get you out of a confusing situation? *Christ is far more reliable than all our electronic inventions and chemical discoveries.* Remember that truth as you go through your everyday activities—when you rely on a water faucet or a telephone or an ibuprofen capsule. If you say to yourself every time you stand up, "I can trust my Lord more than I can depend on this floor to support me," you'll soon find it easy to believe!

2. Express what you believe. We all hear people say, "If you want something done right, do it yourself." They shake their heads and mutter, "You can't depend on anybody nowadays." You may catch them by surprise if you counter with, "Except God." Go ahead and startle

them! One way to really establish your beliefs in your own heart is to articulate them to someone else. If you actually come out and tell a mumbler, "I believe God is trustworthy, and He has ways of working things out that are far beyond what I could possibly imagine. If anyone is dependable, it's God," you'll certainly have to believe that for yourself too.

3. Create "I believe" signs. Sometimes when our situations seem the bleakest, we need to be bombarded with the facts. Make yourself several signs that assert what you believe about God. Hang an "I believe God is merciful" sign on your car's rearview mirror; tack "I believe God provides" on your refrigerator; tape "I believe God cares about me" on your bathroom mirror. Pick a promise you really need to remember and carry a copy of it in your wallet so you'll see it over and over again. Those constant reminders of God's wonderful characteristics may be just what it takes to get you through a maze of a day.

4. Memorize the Nicene or the Apostles' Creed. These ancient descriptions of the tenets of our faith were written by early

Christians to help them stand up against anything false that may have been trying to infiltrate the Church. We can hold onto them when times get confusing and we're not sure what to think or where to go. Many people recite one or the other each Sunday in their worship services, but if you've never bothered to commit one of them to memory, do so now. These truths about God, which have been foundations of the Church for many generations, can be concrete facts to bear in mind when everything else you believe in seems vague. Following is the Apostles' Creed, believed to be the older of the two creeds:

"We believe in God, the Father almighty, creator of heaven and earth.

"We believe in Jesus Christ, his only Son, our Lord. He was conceived by the power of the Holy Spirit and born of the Virgin Mary. He suffered under Pontius Pilate, was crucified, died, and was buried. He descended to the dead. On the third day He rose again. He ascended into heaven, and is seated at the right hand of the Father. He will come again to judge the living and the dead.

"We believe in the Holy Spirit, the holy catholic Church, the communion of saints, the forgiveness of sins, the resurrection of the body, and the life everlasting. Amen."

5. Send an "I believe" letter to another person. Even though it's difficult to see God's will in our own lives, many times we can easily see the good He wants for others. Since everyone loves to receive personal mail, try writing a letter of encouragement to your pastor who needs a vacation; to your friend who is feeling lonely; to your daughter who will be heading off to college in the fall. Send personal messages reminding the recipients that Christ is leading them onward in life, and that He has some wonderful plans. Describe the good qualities you've noticed God has given them—especially the ones that might help them through the confusions they are facing. Then, when you're through writing, look back over your letters. Which of those gifts that you've outlined has God also given to you? If the Lord is making a way for them, why wouldn't He be just as happy to make a way for you? Imagine that Christ were writing you this kind of letter.

What would He say to you? Choose to believe it.

Especially for Families

6. Play the A-B-C game. This is a fun thing to do with children in the car or around the table at mealtime. Each person names a characteristic of God that begins with the sequential letter of the alphabet. You might start out, "I believe God is *A*ccepting." The person next to you says, "I believe God is *B*ig." Then, "I believe God is *C*aring. I believe God is *D*ependable. I believe God is *E*ternal," etc.

7. Go on a nature walk. Take your children outside to see what clues God has given us about Himself. Notice the hundreds of different kinds of trees: God has an incredible imagination. Listen to the songs of the birds: God enjoys music. Look at the uniqueness of each snowflake: God pays attention to small details. Help your kids discover the fun of learning about God through what He's created. Then read them these words of Jesus: "Are not five sparrows sold for two pennies? Yet not one of them is forgotten by God. Indeed, the very hairs of your head are all numbered.

Don't be afraid; you are worth more
than many sparrows" (Lk. 12:6-7).

8. Compose an "I believe" song. Children
learn so much from music—why not use
it to teach them to trust the Lord? Perhaps a favorite nursery rhyme or a Dis-
ney tune can provide a melody for your
"family song." Make the words simple
so the point really comes across. Here's
an example, to be sung to the tune of
"Row, Row, Row Your Boat":

> I, I, I believe
> Christ will make a way.
> He'll help
> you, too—
> Trust in God today.

Chapter 2

A Promise-Filled Bible

The sports editor of the old *New York Globe* wanted his daily cartoon. The year was 1918, and the 25-year-old illustrator who was responsible for the job searched desperately for an idea.

Rummaging through his files—sports oddities he had collected through the years for his own amusement—he found the following:

- M. PAULIQUEN, Paris 1912, remained under water 6 minutes, 29-4/5 seconds.
- A. FORRESTER of Toronto ran 100 yards backwards in 14 seconds.

He drew simple figures to depict these and other facts because that's all he could come up with to meet his looming deadline.

Entitling the page "Champs or Chumps," the young man wasn't all that sure he had done a good piece of work. Maybe a different title would help. Crossing out the first attempt, he quickly lettered in "Believe It or Not!" and left the cartoon on his editor's desk.

Not thinking about it any further, the artist went across the street for a cup of coffee, never imagining he had struck upon an idea that would capture the imagination of millions of readers and make "Believe It or Not" a household phrase all over the world.

The next day the rough cartoon appeared in the *Globe* and readership response was immediate and positive. So Robert Ripley was asked to do a similar piece as soon as he could get the material. In time, "Believe It or Not" appeared weekly, then twice a week, and finally every day. Other papers received permission to publish the material, and before long the feature was syndicated in more than 300 papers, 38 countries, and 17 languages, with an amazing readership of 80 million.

In time, newspaper tycoon William Randolph Hearst became a sponsor, and Ripley traveled the world looking for stories. The Duke of Windsor called him "the modern Marco Polo."

Ripley's books and collections of curios became increasingly popular. They were also startlingly accurate. Distinguished radio journalist Lowell Thomas commented on this in the foreword of one of Ripley's illustrated editions:

"The day after Lindbergh made his historic trans-Atlantic flight in 1927, Ripley's newspaper cartoon announced that Lindbergh was the 67th person to make this nonstop journey by air from America to Europe. This, naturally, drew an avalanche of protests—more than 3000 letters and telegrams poured in from irate readers. Of course, what Lindbergh had achieved was the first across-the-Atlantic **solo** flight; Alcock and Brown had been the first, in 1919. The English dirigible **R34** had made the flight with 31 aboard the same year, and the German **ZR** (later the **Los Angeles**) crossed in 1924 with 33 passengers. Ripley was right again...and those who had been so quick to protest became Ripley fans."

Ripley's books are replete with odd historical facts like this one: "General Henry Heth (1825-1888), leading a Confederate division in the battle of Gettysburg, was hit in the head by a Union bullet. But his life was saved because he was wearing a hat two sizes too large, with newspaper folded inside the sweatband. The paper deflected the bullet and the general, unconscious for 30 hours, recovered and lived another 25 years."

Believe it or not!

Of course, the possibility of truth being stranger than fiction is what made these items interesting. A reader had to decide, "Am I going to believe this? No way! But then, Ripley says it's true!"

A far more important set of truths is found in another unique volume. I personally have never seen anything to match it. Once again the reader is forced to decide, "Am I going to believe this?"

Like Ripley's *Believe It or Not*, this uncommon book was also compiled over a period of years, and the stories come from various nations. The nature of it is different than Ripley's work because these truths reportedly represent the mind of God. Included in its many pages are phenomenal promises that the reader must decide upon. Are they believable or aren't they?

Now, few people have trouble believing promises until push comes to shove. Perhaps your brother assures you that you can borrow his van to go on vacation. The test is whether or not he'll come through when you say, "I want it the second week of June; that's when I plan to drive to Santa Fe." When the date of departure rolls closer, his wife, your sister-in-law, might begin to have second thoughts about the offer. Will his promise hold up?

Maybe your best friend mentioned the loan of her designer gown for that formal company dinner at which you will be receiving a reward. But as the gala night approaches, you sense some hesitancy. "You're really a size larger," she says...

Strange as it may seem, a good time to put the promises of Scripture to the test is during those awkward occasions when we're maneuvering our way through a maze of one kind or another. That's when we are less self-confident than we might normally be, so we're not able to cover for God if He doesn't come through.

Let's work with this example. First Corinthians 10:13 says: "No temptation has seized you except what is common to man. And God is faithful; He will not let you be tempted beyond what you can bear. But when you are tempted, He will also provide a way out so that you can stand up under it."

That's a great promise when everything is going well and you're on top of the world. It's not quite as delightful when you're caught in a corporate downscaling, or the doctoral dissertation committee disapproves of the thesis topic that really excites you, or the brakes go out on the used car—again—or you're publicly criticized by opponents, or you're facing terminal illness or a debilitating disease, or you're not achieving what you expected in a chosen field of endeavor.

"God will not let you be tempted beyond what you can bear." Come on—when life's a bummer, we have every reason to give in to temptation and halfway blame God for our actions under pressure. Right?

Here's the real test for when you decide whether you'll believe it or not. Do you really embrace this promise from the Bible that no temptation has seized you except what's common to men and women? Are you truly convinced that God is faithful, and that He won't let you be tempted beyond what you can bear?

Or do you give in, like the young college professor Charles van Doren does in the Robert Redford movie *Quiz Show*? His temptation is to become the new intellectual genius and win all the prize money, even though he quickly learns that the quiz show is rigged and they're feeding him the questions and answers ahead of time. That's certainly beyond most young men's ability to pass up...isn't it? So what good is such an ancient verse about a unique and modern temptation being common to man, and God not allowing him to be tempted beyond what he can bear?

At another time in history, another young man said, "I choose to believe the promises. I'll bank my life on what the Scriptures say."

In this situation the man under pressure was physically weak. He hadn't eaten for 40 days. Mentally he was working his way through a huge transition from being an unknown tradesman to announcing his rightful kingship.

"You're obviously hungry," satan pointed out. "Why not just tell these stones here to become bread, croissants, muffins, or even Parker House rolls?"

Christ's mind immediately considered: What do the Scriptures say? "It is written," He quoted to His tempter, " 'Man does not live on bread alone, but on every word that comes from the mouth of God.' " He distinctly gave the impression that He hardly thought much about what the enemy was saying. In His mind the only consideration was, what does God say? What's in the Scriptures?

Then the devil took Him to Jerusalem, "Look, it's time to announce who You are. Do it with dramatic flair. Throw Yourself off the highest point of the temple. You want a reminder of what the Bible says? Well, it reads, 'He will command His angels concerning you, and they will lift you up in their hands.'"

Christ immediately replied, "It is also written: 'Do not put the Lord your God to the test.'"

This series of conflicts revolves around two questions: What does the Word of the Lord say? And, what's appropriate for this immediate troubling situation?

Satan again said: "Let me show You what I can give You if You will bow down and worship me."

Bad move. Too obvious. "Away from Me," snapped our Lord. "For it is written: 'Worship the Lord your God, and serve Him only.'"

In some ways, this scenario in Matthew 4 is like a "battle of the book." "This is My Father's Word, and I must choose whether to believe it or not!"

You're in trouble when a similar dramatic scene presents itself and you let the battle shift away from the written Word and its promises. "I'll tell you what, satan," you might say, "Go over that temptation one more time. I just want to review your offer." Forget it then! Such equivocation is a sure sign that you are wading in deep waters.

No temptation has taken you but such as is common to man. God is faithful; He will not allow you to be tempted above what you're able. Do you believe it, or not?

A similar promise is in Second Peter 1:3-4.

> *His divine power has given us everything we need for life and godliness through our knowledge of Him who called us by His own glory and goodness. Through these He has given us His very great and precious promises, so that through them you may participate in the divine nature and escape the corruption in the world caused by evil desires.*

Once again, believe it or not!

Embracing these promises is what carries people through confusing times, not only in terms of overcoming the enemy (who can be expected to attack most frequently when we are weak), but also in regard to giving us handholds when we're in a dense fog. "I'm confused, Lord; I'm bewildered. Life has suddenly become much too complex."

Another promise is from the mouth of the One who always lived by God's promises: "Ask and it will be given to you; seek and you will find; knock and the door will be opened to you. For everyone who asks receives; he who seeks finds; and to him who knocks, the door will be opened" (the words of Christ in Matthew 7:7-8).

"Yeah," someone jokes, "but I don't like it when I knock and it takes forever for the person to come and open the door." What do humorous comments like this really mean? I think they suggest that we really don't believe the promise!

Once again, this is the basic question with which we must wrestle when lost in one of life's labyrinths: Do I believe God's Word or not? Yes or no?

"I believe it," you say.

Good.

In the Old Testament, the people of Israel wandered around 40 years more than they needed to because they responded to God's believe-it-or-not question with national waffling.

God's promises were true then. He never failed His people, though they continually failed their God. Joshua 21:43 and 45 tell the end of the story: "So the Lord gave Israel all the land He had sworn to give their forefathers, and they took possession of it and settled there. ... Not one of all the Lord's good promises to the house of Israel failed; every one was fulfilled."

A good time to embrace—to hug tightly to your soul—the great promises of God's Word is precisely when you're trying to maneuver your way through a wilderness maze. That's another key scriptural truth I'm learning to live with. In a sentence, I'm saying that *a good time to embrace the great promises of God's Word is when trying to maneuver through a maze.*

Life isn't designed by God to be like it was for Bill Murray in the movie *Ground Hog Day* where, if you make a mistake, you have to relive that same day over and over until you finally figure out how to do it right. But even though we aren't stuck in a time warp, many people do repeat their mistakes over and over—mistakes as basic as assuming they can affirm the truth of Scripture doctrinally, while repeatedly denying the promises in practicality. Lifetime mistakes show that in our heart of hearts, we really don't believe that if we ask, it will be given to us; if we seek, we'll find; if we knock, God will open the door.

On the other hand, "I believe" people—the people who practice making "I believe" statements—declare, "If I'm knocking and the door hasn't opened, I'll knock louder. If I'm asking and God hasn't granted my request, I must not be asking quite right. Because I know the promise doesn't read that everyone who asks receives—NOT!" If a son asks for bread, is he going to get a stone? If he requests a fish, will he be given a snake? The implied answer is an extremely strong "no!" (See Matthew 7:9-11.)

One additional dilemma many Christians wrestle with is almost a universal maze: Where do I fit in God's plan?

Scripture offers believe-it-or-not statements that relate to this. Remember Philippians 1:4-6:

> *In all my prayers for all of you, I always pray with joy because of your partnership in the gospel from the first day until now, being confident of this, that He who began a good work in you will carry it on to completion until the day of Christ Jesus.*

Do you believe it, or not? Do you really believe that He who began a good work in you will carry it on to completion? Does that belief make you confident? As life unfolds, will God show you where your partnership in the gospel is? Or will He purposely cloud that issue in great mystery and puzzlement?

In Scripture, stewards were servants who had been elevated to positions of high responsibility in their master's household. They were almost always slaves, but not menial slaves. Stewards had to know the desires of their masters. They didn't think, "What do I want," but "What does my lord want done?" The follow-up, but lesser question was, "What are my skills, and how do they equip me to accomplish my master's desires?" A steward was skating on thin ice when too much time was spent considering his skills (or gifts) and not enough time concentrating on his master's wishes.

The apostle Paul wrote: "This is how one should regard us, as servants of Christ and stewards of the mysteries of God. Moreover it is required of stewards that they be found trustworthy" (1 Cor. 4:1-2 RSV).

If you are struggling through the maze of life's calling, consider this first: *What is my Master about, and how can I plug into the agenda He is designing?* Don't try to solve things for 20 years down the road. But for right now ask, *What is my Master about, and how can I involve my skills in His agenda?* It's not terribly complicated.

When you finish this present life passage, ask the same question about the next stage of living: *What's my Master doing that I can assist Him in, utilizing the skills He's given me?* As you keep at this, *I'm* confident that He who began a good work in you will carry it to completion until the day of Christ!

But the question *you* must answer about this Scripture is this: Do you believe it, or not?

As you think about your response, be aware that Christians in many parts of the world are learning to hold onto promises like this. Picture a young man raised as a Hindu in a small village of India, and who has recently come to faith in Christ. He may be more responsive to what Paul wrote than we are in North America. Though he has no money, he walks many miles to enroll in the nearest Bible school, since that's what God is saying in his heart. The Lord honors his faith and opens other doors in what can only be called a series of miracle stories. As he testifies to these to the glory of the Lord, the faith of his hearers is increased and the Kingdom is advanced in a way we in the West know far too little about.

Sometimes a simple illustration like this is a good one. We most capable humans are too often convinced that we really must know everything about God and His ways. But if someone else was already chosen for the executive position you wanted, praise the Lord! God has another good work for you. The only way He can get you to experience it is by blocking what you wanted. Now is not the time to sulk, complain, withdraw, and totally miss the better thing God is unfolding in your behalf.

Again, as strange as it first sounds, a good time to embrace the great promises of God is when trying to maneuver through a maze. So the next time you read Scripture, I suggest that you look for promises in the passage. Write them down. Begin a life list. Start your own believe-it-or-not collection.

A righteous man may have many troubles, but the Lord delivers him from them all (Psalm 34:19).

Believe it or not.

The Lord is good, a refuge in times of trouble. He cares for those who trust in Him (Nahum 1:7).

Believe it or not.

Boxer Danny London was born deaf and dumb. But after he was hit on the head during a fight in Brooklyn, New York, in 1929, he suddenly found he could both speak and hear (Robert Ripley's *Believe It or Not*).

I suspect that some Christians are more prone to believe Ripley than they are Nahum.

It was Ripley who said, concerning the sources for his popular column, "The mine is inexhaustible." He felt he would never run out of material.

> *If any of you lacks wisdom, he should ask God, who gives generously to all without finding fault, and it will be given to him* (James 1:5).

Believe it or not.

> *For we do not have a high priest who is unable to sympathize with our weaknesses, but we have one who has been tempted in every way, just as we are—yet was without sin* (Hebrews 4:15).

Believe it or not.

> *Dear friends, now we are children of God, and what we will be has not yet been made known. But we know that when He appears, we shall be like Him, for we shall see Him as He is* (1 John 3:2).

Believe it or not.

I could go on quoting God's promises because the truth for you and for me is this: Practically speaking, the mine is inexhaustible.

What to Do

Here are some suggestions to help you live out what you've learned in this chapter.

1. Use the 50-Day Spiritual Adventure *Believe It Or Not Promise Pack*. Carry it around with you so you can pull out a promise whenever you don't know what to do. Figure out key words that will trigger the verses (or their concepts, if you don't have them memorized) in your mind. When someone says, "goodbye," for instance, you might remember that God has said, "Never will I leave you; never will I forsake you" (Heb. 13:5).

2. Memorize a "motto" verse. Do you know someone who has a slogan for every occasion? Grandma might chuckle, "Never disturb a happy child" when your toddler is playing in her flower bed, and somehow, what you thought was a catastrophe becomes a funny little happening. The promises of Scripture can just as easily lighten our circumstances. Learn to feel comfortable applying them wherever they might fit. You might wake up with, "God's mercies are new every morning" (see Lam. 3:22-23), and find yourself

smiling, even if you're not a morning person! The following "I Believe" prayer can help you get started memorizing those scriptural promises. Pray it each day, using a verse that applies to you:

Father,

Sometimes I feel confused and don't understand why things happen the way they do. Yet I believe You love me deeply, and that absolutely nothing is beyond Your control. Help me to live each day with confidence, trusting in the great promises of Your Word. Today I am reminded (this is where you fill in your promise verse). *Thank You for giving me the strength to be an "I believe" person. Amen.*

3. Share a promise with someone. Leave a message on a friend's answering machine, or write out a Scripture verse to pack in brown-bag lunches. Surprise your teenager with a verse written at the top of the next clean page of his algebra notebook, or hide a note card with a promise in your wife's briefcase. Sharing these promises not only encourages others, but also gives you the opportunity to think about them each time you share them.

4. Keep a promise log. Write down any of God's promises that you especially like, and keep track of times you see them fulfilled in your life. A promise log entry might look like this:

Come near to God and He will come near to you (James 4:8a).

Aug. 9   Today I was awfully nervous as I anticipated a meeting with my boss. Some of the people at work have been "stealing time"— going swimming in one guy's pool when they're supposed to be out on sales calls in the afternoon. My boss has been frustrated, for although our sales team seems to be working hard, we aren't making the sales he had expected.

     But what could I do? Be a tattletale? I scorned tattlers when I was a kid—how could I *be* one? Then I remembered this verse: *Come near to God.* I ate lunch in my car so I could be alone enough to pray. After half an hour, I think I really had drawn closer to God, asking Him for wisdom and the right, true, just, pure words.

I honestly felt like God walked right into the boss's office with me. I wasn't even tense as I spoke with him (this is the first time *that's* happened)! God must have been talking for me, because for once I didn't get flustered. I didn't even have to mention names or anything—I just told my boss the situation, and he thanked me and said that cleared up a lot of confusion for him.

It cleared up confusion for me too. It's always easier to trust God when I see He's answered a promise. Wonder why I didn't just really talk with Him about this during the last few heavy-worry days?

5. Reclaim the rainbow. Unfortunately, this symbol of God's promise has become an emblem of the New Age movement. That's too bad, for God said, "I have set My rainbow in the clouds, and it will be the sign of the covenant between Me and the earth. Whenever I bring clouds over the earth and the rainbow appears in the clouds, I will remember My covenant between Me and

you..." (Gen. 9:13-15). When we see a rainbow, we too should remember God's covenant never to flood the earth again. Bear it in mind as an example that God will keep His promises, even the one you might be struggling with believing right now.

6. Search for a "Doubt Buster" Scripture. Take some time to find a Scripture passage or a verse that applies specifically to your situation. It's okay to spend several days or weeks hunting for something just right. But when you find the verse that speaks directly to you, profess it as your own. Put it on the back of a T-shirt, write it in your Bible, have it engraved on a plaque for your office. Do whatever it takes to tuck that promise into the deepest part of your mind—a place far deeper than any doubt that might confuse you.

Especially for Families

7. Play the "Sword Drill" game. First, write down the Scripture references from the *Believe It Or Not Promise Pack* and your Adventure Journal, or go through a Bible concordance to find verses with promises. Pass out a Bible (the Sword of the Lord) to all participants

and caution them not to open it until you've said "Go!" Then, read off one of your Scripture references, reading clearly so everyone can understand. Call out, "One, two, three, GO," and watch everyone scramble to find the verse and read it aloud. The first one to find the verse gets a point (or a prize). Younger children, of course, will be less familiar with the whereabouts of books of the Bible. In that case, hide a verse under one family member's plate at mealtime and recite it together so your young ones can participate in the game with you.

8. Sing songs about God's Word. Concentrate on any song that will remind you where to go for answers when life gets confusing. Your kids might sing, "Every Promise in the Book Is Mine," "The B-I-B-L-E," or "Jesus Loves Me." You too can hum "How Firm a Foundation," "A Mighty Fortress," "Thy Word Is a Lamp Unto My Feet," or a chorus you've learned in church services. If you're stuck without the words to these songs, use the following short hymn written by Christopher Wordsworth. It will be easiest to memorize if you fit the words

to "There's No Place Like Home," or another familiar tune:

> Lord, be thy word my rule;
>   in it may I rejoice;
> thy glory be my aim,
>   thy holy will my choice;
> thy promises my hope;
>   thy providence my guard;
> thine arm my strong support;
>   thyself my great reward.

Chapter 3

Relationships Between Believers

People don't go to Mazeville on purpose. At least, if they have any sense they don't. They usually end up there by accident.

That's what happened to two lost hikers. Rain was pouring down so hard they couldn't see well enough to get to their intended destination. Finding a shelter in the storm, they sat down until daybreak. But they were weary, so they both fell asleep.

What they didn't know was that they had wandered onto the grounds of a giant. Unfortunately, the next morning when the huge owner made his rounds, he found them and took both captive. They politely explained that they were on a journey and were lost, but that didn't make any difference. Because of his size, the travelers were afraid to quarrel with their captor.

"The giant, therefore, drove them before him, and put them into his castle, in a very dark dungeon, nasty and stinking to the spirits of these two men. Here, then, they lay from Wednesday morning till Saturday night, without one bit of bread, or drop of drink, or light, or any to ask how they did; they were, therefore, here in evil case, and were far from friends and acquaintance."

What might sound like an old *Muppet Show* script is really a Christian classic. First printed in 1678, *Pilgrim's Progress* by John Bunyan is still revered by people of the Church. The story continues after the giant's wife advised him to beat these trespassers without mercy.

"So when he arose, he getteth him a grievous crab-tree cudgel, and goes down into the dungeon to them, and there first falls to rating of them as if they were dogs, although they never gave him a word of distaste: then he fell upon them, and beat them fearfully, in such sort that they were not able to help themselves, or to turn them upon the floor. This done he withdraws, and leaves them there to condole their misery, and to mourn under their distress: so all that day they spent their time in nothing but sighs and bitter lamentations."

Intent on getting to the Celestial City, these travelers had unwittingly found their way into a literal giant maze that seemed to have no exits. Left alone, the companions discussed their options. The discouraged one, Christian, cried, "The grave is more easy for me than this dungeon!"

Hopeful, his companion, responded in a manner consistent with his name:

"Who knows but that God, who made the world, may cause that Giant Despair may die, or that, at some-time or other, he may forget to lock us in; or that he may in a short time have another of his fits before us, and may lose the use of his limbs? And if ever that should come to pass again, for my part, I am resolved to pluck up the heart of a man, and try my utmost to get from under his hand."

Later, Giant Despair returned and took them to his castle yard and showed them scattered bones and skulls. "These," he said, "were pilgrims, as you are, once, and they trespassed on my grounds, as you have done; and when I thought fit, I tore them in pieces; and so within ten days I will do you."

Discouragement—how often it waylays spiritual pilgrims when they're trapped in a no-win situation. Then dismay—"To think when we started on this path it seemed so pleasant." Hopelessness—"No one cares. Why should we continue? Nobody asks anymore how we're doing." Despondency—"What difference does it make? Nothing seems worth the effort when life is filled with so much bitterness." Yes, old Giant Despair still stalks these parts. He's such a big fellow, you would think pilgrims would see him coming and run. But that's not always the case. Sometimes Despair gets you before you know it.

Bunyan's book has remained popular, mainly because so many believers relate to the experiences of characters like Christian and Hopeful. They know what it's like to be exhausted from traveling hard, following the leading of the Lord. Many also identify with a story about some awful night when they lost direction, sat down under a strange shelter, and fell asleep where they shouldn't have. Unfortunately, the old giant was out roaming his acres the next morning, and "with a grim and surly voice, he bid them awake."

Once captured by Giant Despair, it's extremely difficult to get free by yourself. Just because you tell depression, "Leave me alone," doesn't mean it will. You may not have the strength to keep asking or searching for ways to escape your dungeon. You need a Hopeful to encourage you, to step in and *do* something, if need be.

Maybe I should pause and ask whether you brought any discouragement with you into this maze of yours. Did someone tell you that you weren't needed or you didn't fit, or did a certain gruff individual treat you like a dog? Do you have someone on your side to counteract those falsehoods?

"Well, on Saturday, about midnight, they began to pray, and continued in prayer till almost break of day.

"Now, a little before it was day, good Christian, as one half amazed, brake out into this passionate speech:—What a fool, quote he, am I, thus to lie in a stinking dungeon, when I may as well walk at liberty! I have a key in my bosom, called Promise, that will, I am persuaded, open any lock in Doubting Castle. Then said Hopeful, That's good news, good brother, pluck it out of thy bosom, and try."

Promise is a good word to convey what Christian suddenly rediscovered. In the context of what I have been writing, he returned to being an "I believe" person. He embraced a great truth of Scripture and, with this promise, tried the dungeon door. The bolt gave as he turned the key; it flew open with ease, and Christian and Hopeful both came out.

> "After that, he went to the iron gate, for that must be opened too, but that lock was desperately hard; yet the key did open it. Then they thrust open the gate to make their escape with speed; but that gate, as it opened, made such a creaking, that it waked Giant Despair, who, hastily rising to pursue his prisoners, felt his limbs to fail, for his fits took him again, so that he could by no means go after them. Then they went on, and came to the King's highway again, and so were safe, because they were out of his jurisdiction."

The two pilgrims escaped from Despair—a feat that might not have been accomplished if Christian had been traveling without Hopeful. You see, finding one's way out of a maze is usually easier for two than it is for one. Scripture concurs with Bunyan on this. Ecclesiastes 4:9-10, 12 reads, "Two are better than one...if one falls down, his friend can help him up. But pity the man who falls and has no one to help him up! ... Though one may be overpowered, two can defend themselves. A cord of three strands is not quickly broken." Here is another proactive answer to the question of what to do when you don't know what to do: *Work at building a support relationship with someone who loves the Lord.*

Proverbs 17:17 tells us, "A friend loves at all times, and a brother is born for adversity." In the next chapter, Proverbs 18:24 adds, "A man of many companions may come to ruin, but there is a friend who sticks closer than a brother."

A beautiful Old Testament example of the kind of friendship where one sticks closer than a brother is seen in the relationship between Jonathan and David, God's anointed king-in-waiting. Though he was the prince, Jonathan was loyal to David in every way.

> *And Saul's son Jonathan went to David at Horesh and helped him find strength in God. "Don't be afraid," he said. "My father Saul will not lay a hand on you. You will be*

*king over Israel, and I will be second
to you. Even my father Saul knows
this"* (1 Samuel 23:16-17).

How's that for an example of a friend
who sticks closer than a brother? Jonathan
was certainly one born to be there for
David, offering him hope even in a time of
adversity.

The exact opposite of this scene is por-
trayed in the children's film *The Lion King*,
which grossed over $300 million at the box
office. One lesson young watchers hopefully learn is that when things go wrong,
you shouldn't withdraw from your friends.
Remember how young Prince Simba was
told a lie by his evil Uncle Scar? Because of
this lie, the young lion assumed it was his
fault that his father, Mufasa, died. Simba
ran away from the lion pride. Certainly his
young lioness friend, Nala, could have
helped him think through what went on,
but Simba leaves without even talking to
her. He withdraws to a distant place.

Eventually he makes new friends, but
what's a future king of the jungle doing
running around with a warthog, Pumbaa,
and a meerkat, Timon, whose joint life phi-
losophy is expressed in the song "Haku-
namatata"..."no worries for the rest of our
days"? Not the best of advice, is it? But

don't Christians sometimes face tough problems by withdrawing from everyone—including the people of the King? They forfeit their unique heritage because they fail to hold to the close Christian friendships that are needed. It's as if they drop their royal relationships in favor of no-worry warthogs and meerkats.

Three young men a long way from home in another land also could have formed the wrong kind of friendships if they hadn't been careful. The new surroundings in Babylon were mesmerizing. This was giant territory of a different sort. Ninety feet high and nine feet wide—that's how big the gold statue was that King Nebuchadnezzar made of himself. His decree was that when the royal musicians began playing, everyone was to bow. Separated from each other, Shadrach, Meshach, and Abednego might have capitulated. As a threesome, they were not to be intimidated. Again, when struck in the Mazevilles of Babylon or other countries, it's wise to pursue support relationships with other believers. The thought might not sound all that profound, but it is!

Can you name some friends you would quickly go to when trouble surfaces? I'm not talking about people you would like to speak with if you could make an appointment, but those you could easily ask for help because a relationship has been built over a period of time.

One of the great benefits of close Christian friendships is that together you can go to the true King with your problems. That was what Christian and Hopeful did on that Saturday at midnight. They began to pray and continued until almost the break of day. Tremendous spiritual power is unleashed when two believers go to the Lord in prayer. The Son of God said, in Matthew 18:18-20:

> *I tell you the truth, whatever you bind on earth will be bound in heaven, and whatever you loose on earth will be loosed in heaven. Again, I tell you that if two of you on earth agree about anything you ask for, it will be done for you by My Father in heaven. For where two or three come together in My name, there am I with them.*

A lesson I am learning from brothers and sisters in Third World countries is that they have a deeper belief in the efficacy of prayer than I do. I can use Christian and Hopeful as a sermon illustration. But I know little about praying from midnight through the early morning hours like they did.

In India, however, all-night prayer meetings are common. In the Third World the Church has limited resources, but it has learned to compensate by becoming more dependent on the Lord. A great percentage of Indian believers are comfortable with the New Testament lifestyle in which "praying without ceasing" is just the normal way to live.

For instance, I recall an incident I used to laugh about. Now it makes me embarrassed. On one of my trips to India I went to the studios of Gospel for Asia to record a radio broadcast with two of my associates. From past instances, I was aware of how difficult it is to capture in a short quarter-hour program the diverse cultural experiences you have been taking in. I wanted my listeners to be able to see what I was seeing and to be encouraged by some of the obvious work of the Holy Spirit taking place under the leadership of the Indian Church.

The three of us sat at a table in the recording room. We talked together about what we would say and how we would fit it all into the short amount of airtime we had. I nodded to the Indian engineer behind the glass. He smiled back. We proceeded with the recording, and it went beautifully. For people who are not acquainted with the difficulties of an unscripted three-man discussion, you might not be able to appreciate how difficult that is.

"Great job, you two," I said. "Praise the Lord, He really helped us." Then I addressed the engineer who had been watching everything intently. "Thanks for your help," I told him.

"No problem," he responded in the beautiful English these people learned from the British who ruled them for so many years. "Now we pray, and then we record."

I looked at my fellow workers. Could it be true that what we felt so good about hadn't been taped?

The engineer was still smiling. "First we pray, and then we record," he said again. Apparently this was an important routine he had been taught and he wasn't about to change it for just any visiting minister.

"First we pray, and then we record." There were to be no exceptions. Yes, the comment was humorous. But I also hear the words as a challenge from God: "David, you're too busy—you're foolishly rushing into things. How could you suppose that your early morning private minutes in prayer automatically cover the entire day?" The reminder was a good one. Why hadn't it seemed natural to us as Christian friends and fellow workers to pray before recording?

Coming back to our Western culture, I would say that setting up a short-term prayer partnership with someone would be a good way to learn about the value of Christian support relationships. This is a relatively easy thing to do, and the benefits far outweigh any slight intimidation you might feel. Who is someone you might ask to do that with you? Could you meet once a week for eight or ten times?

If you've never known the experience of praying with someone else, what a treat is in store for you! The second best time to initiate such a practice is when you're struggling to get out of a maze. Are the problems you face big enough that you're not quite sure how to act or what to do? An obvious suggestion of what to do is to pray. But don't pray on your own! Instead, develop a relationship with someone who will consistently meet with you for prayer. It's much better that way.

Sometimes I think the Lord actually allows us to get into situations over our heads to almost force us to grab hold of others for support. It's as if He's telling us, "There's a reason I sent My disciples out

two by two. Especially when they were as-
signed places of ministry like Mazeville!"

Over the years I have found involve-
ment in prayer partnerships to be one of
my greatest sources of strength. I have
prayed with friends who have been struggling to find their way. I have also been the
recipient of similar prayers. I can remember driving away from prayer times wondering how others who don't have prayer
partners to stand with them make it
through life.

I'm convinced that the best time to consider experimenting with a prayer partnership is when all is going well. Then you
have opportunity to spend time praising
God for His goodness. You can learn a great
deal about praying with a friend if you
don't have to hit the road running, so to
speak. The pressure isn't there to expect
God to perform an incredible miracle between meeting one and meeting two!

It's also helpful to make a distinction
between going to someone for prayer support and meeting with someone for coun-
seling. When the initial meetings are
problem-oriented, there is always the
temptation for more time to be spent in
sharing advice than in prayer. The purpose
of prayer times is to present your problems

to the Lord with a friend by your side act-
ing as an intercessor for you.

A book I coauthored with Steve Bell,
called *Two Are Better Than One*, says it
well:

> "Within a short time after enter-
> ing a prayer partnership, normally
> you will see improvement in your
> private time with the Lord. Spend-
> ing time with someone else in the
> presence of God enhances personal
> times with Him. You become prac-
> ticed and more comfortable in His
> presence. Talking with the Lord
> about specific issues in your life no
> longer seems so abstract. On top of
> that, many have testified that the
> promises of Scripture come alive to
> them in a whole new way. What had
> become the drudgery of doing basic
> spiritual disciplines has trans-
> formed into a new spiritual vitality.

> "Finally, the church stands in
> great need of praying people. Pastors
> want the prayer support of their
> members. Those in the congregation
> have all kinds of heart-breaking re-
> quests. Few outsiders come to Christ
> if nobody is praying for them. And

spiritual awakenings always require
a prayer base."

Christian and Hopeful needed each
other. Apparently Jonathan and David did
too. The cord of three strands, Shadrach,
Meshach, and Abednego, was not quickly
broken.

Maybe you feel you can make it on your
own.

I don't think I can...at least not while
I'm here in Mazeville!

What to Do

Here are some suggestions to help you live out what you've learned in this chapter.

1. Practice hospitality. A great way to develop relationships with other Christians is to invite them to your house. Conversation seems to take off over a home-cooked meal or around a crackling fireplace. So free your Sunday afternoons for a time when you can get together with one or a few of God's people. Don't worry about being fancy; concern yourself with making them feel comfortable. It only takes a few well-thought-out words to prompt a shy person to open up. If you feel at ease with the person, talk about the possibilities of praying together. Both you and your friend may find a needed comrade in spiritual warfare.

2. Get plugged into a church. It may seem obvious, but this is one of the best places to go in times of confusion. The Body of Christ is full of imperfect people just like you who don't always know what to do. Still, you'll find older and wiser people, enthusiastic young people, teachers, counselors, and plenty of real-life experiences within the church

walls. It's a place of nourishment; go there for your strength.

3. Press past the "gulp factor." When someone tells you about the hard times he or she is going through, it's fine to say, "I'll pray for you." But it's even better to ask, "May I pray for you right now?" Swallow the lump in your throat, push beyond your awkward hesitations, and find a corner of the church or spend a few extra minutes on the phone going directly to the Lord with the problem. Your friend or acquaintance will know that you really are praying, since you've already done so. And you'll get into the practice of supporting others in their confusing times.

4. Start an "Aaron and Hur Society." It's easy to criticize political leaders, bosses, or even pastors while sitting back and doing nothing to help them. However, they may be going through a time of not knowing what to do themselves. Aaron and Hur were two Bible heroes who helped to win a battle—not by doing the fighting, but by holding up Moses' arms of blessing over the soldiers who were at combat for Israel. We can do a similar thing for God's Kingdom by holding up

in prayer the leaders God has placed over us. Find another person who has a heart for revival in the nation and pray for the President. Get together with a coworker or a fellow Sunday school teacher and intercede for your boss or your pastor. You may one day find yourself a hero for the way you've supported those leaders before the Lord.

5. Incorporate your schedule into your praying. If you find that you don't have as much time as you'd like to set aside for prayer with a partner, make use of the routine of your schedule. For instance, if you try to walk a mile every morning for exercise, invite your prayer partner to walk with you. Carpool with a Christian friend who also commutes to work, and pray as you drive. (Nobody said you *have* to pray with your eyes closed!) Watch the six o'clock news "together" on your separate televisions, and spend a few minutes praying over the phone for what's happening in the world and the nation. Pray over the phone while you're both ironing the week's laundry, or ask your partner to help you pray while painting the garage some Saturday. Search for those times in your hectic day that you might be

able to make use of a partner. It'll help your social life as well as your prayer life.

6. Let yourself care. Sometimes we don't have any supportive friendships in our life-mazes because we don't know how to *be* a supportive friend. Many people are hurting so much in their own situations that they can't handle the thought of caring for others in their crises. Not caring can lead to loneliness, and loneliness makes tough circumstances much worse. Try concentrating on someone else's problems for a few minutes each day. Really listen to how he or she is doing. Do what you can to relieve the situation, or simply try to bring a bright spot to his or her day. You may notice that when you think about another person's problems, you give God a chance to take care of your own. Even if it seems that He doesn't fix them right away, you've taken another step toward developing a supportive friendship.

Especially for Families

7. Partner up with your kids. Schedule a time when you can be a prayer partner to your children. They need to be able to

unload their frustrations and confusions too; develop the habit of praying with them about those mazes in their lives. Be objective; don't give too much advice; try not to judge them. (It may be helpful to follow the instructions on page 34 in your Adventure Journal.) If you'd like, you can also team your ten-year-old daughter with her four-year-old brother. Older kids can be wonderful role models for youngsters, and praying with little Timmy will put her in a role that will help her mature spiritually. Take these times seriously—your kids will!

8. Play group games. Since most of us have a certain degree of natural independence, both young and old need to understand how important it is to lean on each other. Many games have been created to teach appropriate interdependence, and we all could stand a fun-filled reminder. Invite some of your children's classmates over for a fun afternoon, or plan a night of coffee and hors d'oeuvres for your small group. Check out a book of games from your local library (or if you're really creative, make some up!) and have a fun-filled time of learning.

Chapter 4

Refreshing Joys

It was such a simple question from a friend. "Hi, how are you doing?" What made you come unglued like you did?

Maybe it was because she always looks great—fabulous clothes, money for a hairstylist and manicurist—and you're pushing like everything just to buy gym shoes for the kids.

Or maybe you're a man who's behind on the house payments; financial catastrophe seems to be around every corner. It's like real life has become a game of Monopoly in which you don't own a single property—not even one of the railroads—and you're down to your last $10.

In high school you were on top of the heap. What happened to your life? You thought you had great potential, that your future was bright with promise!

Out of shape physically? Yeah. Who has time to exercise? What about spiritually? Out of shape there too. After all, who has time for devotions? Socially? Pretty desperate. But again, when you don't feel good about yourself, why make extra efforts to build friendships, practice hospitality, or join a prayer group or Bible study?

How are you doing? Such a simple question. But when these maze-times come, if we're honest we answer: "I'm filled with fear, okay? Yeah, fear! Fear that I'll fail, fear that I'll disappoint people. Fear I'll be rejected, fear I won't amount to anything, fear I'll never become what I was intended to be...even fear because this stupid world is in such a mess, a bigger mess than anyone can make sense out of. I'm extremely uncertain, I'm sad, and I'm growing cynical.

"How am I doing? Okay, I'm a Christian, so everything's supposed to be fine... even though it's not. Life's really a puzzle, an unsolvable conundrum, a cursed maze I'm lost in!"

Living in maze conditions has been my personal experience this excruciating past year. As an honest man, I almost prefer that people not ask me how I'm doing. No, I don't answer negatively like I've suggested. I intentionally practice speaking words that affirm that I am still an "I

believe" person. That's been a good practice
for my soul. But words don't pay radio bills
or satisfy station owners who choose to believe what critics write about the Mainses.

I have, nevertheless, tenaciously held
onto the great promises of God's Word. *Believe it or not*, I've told myself. In the process, what has changed most have been my
thoughts and my expressions.

Like Job, I have cried out:

> *How I long for the months gone by,
> for the days when God watched over
> me, when His lamp shone upon my
> head and by His light I walked
> through darkness! Oh, for the days
> when I was in my prime, when God's
> intimate friendship blessed my house,
> ... when my path was drenched with
> cream and the rock poured out for me
> streams of olive oil. When I went to
> the gate of the city and took my seat
> in the public square, the young men
> saw me and stepped aside and the
> old men rose to their feet; ... Whoever
> heard me spoke well of me, and those
> who saw me commended me, ... I
> thought, "I will die in my own house,
> my days as numerous as the grains
> of sand. My roots will reach to the
> water, and the dew will lie all night*

on my branches." ... *But now they mock me, men younger than I, whose fathers I would have disdained to put with my sheep dogs* (Job 29:2-4, 6-8,11,18-19; 30:1).

"I've also been in the middle of a muddle that won't end," you say. "It's a quagmire—a baffling, confounding, perplexing maze. And I need help to know what to do when I don't know what to do."

Here, then, is another scriptural truth that is guiding my behavior: *A good thing to do when you don't know what to do is to take note of the joys that refresh your spirit.*

Let me explain. Sometimes beleaguered people refuse to smile at all until they're totally out of the maze. That's not good, for it could be a long time before freedom is your lot.

I've found it helpful to chronicle the good things in my journal, to look for simple joys, believing they are always present in my days.

Dec. 3   Thanks, Lord, for a good evening with my son Joel and daughter-in-law Laurie. That play, *The Quilters*, was a great choice for us, and the Japanese restaurant we went to after the performance was delightful.

Dec. 9   Just found out that our new religious TV show, "You Need to Know," was nominated for Television Program of the Year by the National Religious Broadcasters. What a surprise! We're one of two finalists—that's great!

Dec. 14   A will came in today for $8,000; that really helps The Chapel Ministries. Bless You, Lord, and please thank this good person who is now with You.

Did you see the popular film, *Forrest Gump*? The main character, Forrest Gump, was adept at seeing the good in everything. A contemporary holy fool, I think his attraction for an often dissipated and jaded American viewing audience was this capability of positive innocence.

Reading Scripture recently, I began to picture Ruth as a kind of female Forrest Gump. To start with, she doesn't really know God any more than the film hero does. She's married to a Jew who dies on her like Forrest's wife does on him. Remember Gump's line in the movie? "Mother says dying is a part of living. I wish it weren't!"

When Naomi, the older widow, decides to return home to who-knows-what, Ruth's sister-in-law stays in Moab where she's always lived. Ruth, however, clings to Naomi and says, "Where you go I will go...." (Can you hear her sounding a little like a female Forrest?) "Your people will be my people and your God my God" (Ruth 1:16).

When the two reach Bethlehem, it's barley harvest time and Ruth gleans with the poor folk behind the professional reapers. And wouldn't you know it, she's innocently chosen the field of wealthy Boaz, a relative of Naomi's.

Noticing her, a beautiful young stranger, he invites her to share his lunch. "What a nice man," she tells her mother-in-law, who by now has figured out who this powerful landowner is.

"When he lies down," Naomi instructs Ruth, "note the place. Then go and uncover his feet and lie down. He will tell you what to do."

"I will do whatever you say," responds Ruth Gump, or pardon, Ruth from Moab.

Perhaps for the sake of contemporaneousness, I'm not being fair to this woman whose name appears in Matthew's genealogy of Christ. But in the middle of a hard time, she has this marvelous quality of always finding what is good, and I want to be like her in the middle of my hard times.

Dec. 16   Office Christmas party is wonderful. What a great staff of loyal workers You have given me, Lord. And how good to laugh together.

Dec. 18   Enjoyed the time at the Neff's open house. Thank You for friends who show love in beautiful ways.

When the going is rough, social occasions can sometimes give us a needed change of pace. This was true in the scriptural passage I want to refer to next. It's halfway through the final week of Christ's life, and He's aware of everything in the horrific near future. Very soon He will gather with the Twelve to celebrate the Passover one last time. You can feel the pressure building in these historic accounts as Christ orchestrates all events leading to His betrayal, trial, and crucifixion.

But a person can only take so much heaviness; then, in today's terminology, you max out. I thought the Spielberg film, *Schindler's List*, was masterful. If it had been a documentary, it would have been overwhelming. As it was, there were shining moments of good which made it tolerable to take in the magnitude of the evil being chronicled. But audiences needed breaks from the holocaust narrative or it would have been too much to absorb.

Possibly this is what God did for His Son as He faced the final death-defying Jerusalem sequence in Matthew 26. Maybe God the Father provided a respite. Once again, the person who brought the joy that refreshed was a woman. Jesus is reclining at the table in the home of a friend. When this unnamed lady enters the scene, she has an alabaster jar of expensive perfume. Then she pours it over His head.

What an extravagant, fitting, loving act!

Two days before His last Passover, Jesus could have written in His journal: "She poured this marvelous perfume on Me beforehand to prepare for My burial. She didn't even know how significant her 'I-love-you' action was. I told the others in the room that whenever the gospel is preached throughout the world, what she did will be told in her memory. Thank You, Father, for this gift of love and tender care. It touched Me deeply."

Dec. 25   Karen outdid herself fixing Christmas dinner. Dad came, and so did my son Randall, his wife Carmel, and our granddaughter Caitlyn. The other kids were at their in-laws.

Dec. 28   Had dinner with friends who were gentle and kind and sensitive.

Dec. 31   Gaedes clothing store says they will give me four suits a year plus ties if I run a credit line at the end of the TV show. That sure helps!

As I write this, I'm still in the maze. My ministry remains in trouble. Few of my accusers have become silent. I'm still confused about what God is saying to me. Board members are uneasy, and there's always a meeting looming ahead. But I'm determined to keep track of the good. Lord knows I need it!

"Rather, as servants of God we commend ourselves in every way," Paul wrote to the Corinthians, "in great endurance; in troubles, hardships and distresses; in beatings, imprisonments and riots; in hard work, sleepless nights and hunger; ...dying, and yet we live on; beaten, and yet not killed; sorrowful, yet always rejoicing..." (2 Cor. 6:4-5,9-10).

Amazing—"sorrowful, yet always rejoicing." It's hard for me to personally identify with the full impact of Paul's words. But in my travels to other countries, I've met numbers of believers who must know firsthand what he is writing about.

My mind recalls a dinner conversation in the semidarkness of a small hotel/restaurant in South India. Several native missionaries had come to this city for a conference, and that evening they shared their field experiences with me. Their hearts were on fire to reach the lost; they were passionate about planting churches in villages where such a testimony for Christ had never been before. The four at the table told me their stories in broken English. Believe me, their sacrifices were far beyond anything I have ever considered offering to the Lord.

Most knew the rejection of their Hindi parents when as young men they became converts to Christ. With no exceptions they told of being threatened in their ministries, of dodging rocks (or being hit by them), of being tied up and beaten up. They testified about long trips that took them far from those they loved, of often being without funds—sometimes even eating leaves to somehow alleviate their hunger pangs when it got really bad. Of course, they had marvelous stories of God's answering their prayers, of many converts, of getting congregations started, of church buildings being erected, and of the birthing of daughter and granddaughter churches. But all of them knew a friend whose life had been given to advance the cause of Christ.

It was a serious night because these native missionaries were wholeheartedly committed to seeing the Lord work in a powerful way in their land, and they spoke with the same fervency as Paul the apostle did of those they had led to the Lord. Ironically, it was a most pleasurable night as well. The overriding mood was one of joy, optimism, and victory. Laughter was not infrequent, in spite of the fact that we didn't always understand each other's words. Here were determined young workers on special missions for Christ, but also men who totally enjoyed what they were doing. They truly viewed their dangers as the least they could expect, considering who they served and how for centuries the enemy had opposed what they were now doing.

To my knowledge, none of them saw the evening as out of place—an unnecessary diversion. My guess is that they seldom if ever ate at a hotel, although by Western standards the building we were in was hardly large enough to merit the term. But I assume they welcomed the opportunity and probably thanked the Lord for it, seeing the time as a brief break from the activities at hand so they could share what

God was doing with a minister from the United States.

For me, it was a night I'll not forget. I can still picture the surroundings, see the faces, hear the voices, and even recapture some of the immense joy that marked that time together.

"Be joyful always," Paul wrote to the Thessalonians. "Give thanks in all circumstances, for this is God's will for you in Christ Jesus" (1 Thess. 5:16,18). They understood what he had in mind.

When the journey is difficult, the mission confusing, the way fraught with dangers, I choose to believe that the Lord will provide items or occasions of refreshment and ministry for me. I must learn to make the most of them.

Not long after I graduated from Wheaton, Tolkien's *Trilogy of the Ring* came out. Reading the 1,359 pages of these three volumes was like taking a postgraduate course in fantasy adventure literature.

Most readers are familiar with the story of the intrepid band of nine, including Frodo the Hobbit, who must take the one Ring, ruler of all the Rings of power, and destroy it in the stronghold of evil Sauron. There are so many pages of difficult encounters, long journeys, injuries, confusing twists and turns, and of course, frightening battles.

For the reader, it's most refreshing at the end of Book One when the nine adventurers come to Lothlorien, where the elves reign.

> "They remained some days in Lothlorien, so far as they could tell or remember. All the while that they dwelt there the sun shone clear, save for a gentle rain that fell at times, and passed away leaving all things fresh and clean. The air was cool and soft, as if it were early spring, yet they felt about them the deep and thoughtful quiet of winter. It seemed to them that they did little but eat and drink and rest, and walk among the trees; and it was enough."

Everyone who journeys through life's terrible pilgrimages needs such breaks. We have to be refreshed in our arduous passages. Certainly we must not overlook these delightful provisions or let them slip through our fingers. Here's my real-world Lothlorien list:

Jan. 2   First workday of the new year; excellent mail from friends

Jan. 6   Have been sick and my voice gives out doing TV taping. My cohost, Melissa Timberlake, fills in at the last minute and does a great job. I'm proud of her.

Jan. 9   Board meets, but at the last minute three people have to cancel, for legitimate reasons. First time in 19 years we don't have a quorum. No official meeting is held. Takes the pressure for decisions off for the moment. They'll try to get together again a month from now. Overall picture should be much better by then, so praise the Lord!

In Scripture it's a terrible day in Israel's history, a time of lamenting because Jerusalem had fallen, when Jeremiah wrote in Lamentations 3:19-23:

I remember...the bitterness and the gall. ...and my soul is downcast within me. Yet this I call to mind and therefore I have hope: because of the Lord's great love we are not consumed, for His compassions never fail. They are new every morning...

That was from a man whose country had just been conquered.

Are you yourself in a maze? Can you af firm, "God's compassion is new every morning"? Can you sing the old hymn, truly believing?

"Great is thy faithfulness,
O God my Father,
there is no shadow of turning with thee;
thou changest not, Thy compassions,
    they fail not;
As thou hast been thou forever wilt be.
'Great is thy faithfulness!
Great is thy faithfulness!'
Morning by morning new mercies I see;
All I have needed
    thy hand hath provided—
'Great is thy faithfulness,'
Lord, unto me!"

Jan. 16   A letter arrives informing me that we have won the award of 1995 Television Program of the Year by vote of the constituency of the National Religious Broadcasters. The announcement and trophy will be presented at the opening session of the NRB Convention in Nashville at the Opreyland auditorium. That's fabulous news!

Great is Thy faithfulness, Lord, unto me.

Without a doubt, I haven't yet negotiated all the passageways in my present personal maze. I sense I'm getting closer to solving it. But in the process, I am learning about what to do when I don't know what to do. Again, one important item is to take note of the joys that refresh my spirit. And I heartily commend the practice to you.

No, it's not an original idea. I defer to Jeremiah and to Ruth and to Paul and to many others who have gone before me. Every one of these people would testify that God brings His grace to bear even in the midst of our trials.

What to Do

Here are some suggestions to help you live out what you've learned in this chapter.

1. Keep a record of joyful happenings. Tracking the good things that happen throughout the day will encourage you. Your 50-Day Spiritual Adventure Journal contains pages in which you can log your joys; however, if you're not doing the Adventure right now, make a chart in a notebook or pick up a blank page journal at your local drugstore to write in. Describing on paper the joys that pop into your day will help you consciously acknowledge them now and lead you to thankfully reflect on them later.

2. Listen to some "feel good" music. Play Beethoven's "Jesu, Joy of Man's Desiring," or "Morning Has Broken" performed on a Celtic harp, or some other musical piece that makes you smile. It only takes five minutes—get away from any distractions for that short time, and listen to something that brings a little joy to your day.

3. Learn to say "Thank you." Often we come to God with a long list of "I-wishes" and "Please-fix-thises" in our hands. As spiritual as we might make our requests

sound, they need to be balanced with our heartfelt thanks for what God *has* given us. Don't think that just because God is omniscient we don't need to express what we appreciate about Him. He may know, but He still treasures those times when we specifically come to say, "What You did was great!" We can also benefit from recounting those incredible blessings He has imparted. Make your next prayer list a thank-you note.

4. Point to the positive. We all encounter things throughout the day that we'd rather not have to deal with. When you face a tiresome task or a difficult situation, find one thing—no matter how far-fetched it seems—that you might *like* in the midst of that drudgery. "I hate cleaning my floors, but it sure felt nice to walk on them barefoot!" you might say. Or, "My daughter sure is giving me trouble these days, but at least she looks kind of cute when she's sleeping!" You may hate dealing with numbers, but think how successful you feel when your checkbook is balanced. And despite knowing that you'll have to reject that huge job offer, doesn't it make you proud to know that the company

wanted you? They say "the optimist proclaims that we live in the best of all possible worlds; and the pessimist fears this is true." Why not be a complete optimist, just for one day?

5. Do something you enjoy. Maybe you love gardening, reading, making crafts, cooking, or listening to music. Set aside a reasonable amount of time each day to participate in those activities. If "shop till you drop" is your utmost motto, go out in search of some small gifts for your coworkers or study-group members. Reserve extra time to take care of your appearance, go for a walk, or work out at the gym. Taking a little time to sit in your favorite pleasant spot or to talk with a certain someone can bring great joy and peace to a crazy day.

Especially for Families

6. Learn from your children. "Youth's the season made for joys," wrote poet John Gay. It's true—kids usually find it easier to revel in the good, fun, delightful parts of life than adults do. So take a lesson from them. Listen for your three-year-old's giggle, and find out what's making him so happy. Watch for that sparkle in your second grader's eyes,

and try to participate in her pleasure. Ask your children, "What was fun about today?" as you tuck them into bed. Seemingly insignificant things can bring your youngsters joy. Why not let them bring you a needed dose of bliss too?

7. Watch for "Joy Spots" in your day. Whenever something good happens, recognize it and tell someone else about it. If you have children, teach them to call out, "Joy Spot!" when they're happy about something that's happened—or even when they're just feeling good for no particular reason. Make sure you pay close attention to the "Joy Spots" other people describe to you. Ask for specifics about what made them feel good, and rejoice along with them.

8. Make up an "Amusing Mementos" book. Keep track of the things your children say that you might find funny someday. If your three-year-old calls out "Me too! Me too!" every time you kiss your wife, write it down. If your little girl habitually lifts her arms and says, "I'll hold you" when she wants to be picked up, or your youngest son innocently sighs, "Amen" when the pastor's prayer is too long, get those comical events down on

paper. Make up a computer file for your
stories, or stick them in a scrapbook.
They're guaranteed to bring fond memories and chuckles both now and in the future. They'll even provide a cherished
gift for a graduation or wedding day!

Chapter 5

Living Free
From Confusion

One of my all-time favorite comedy films came out in 1991. It stars Richard Dreyfuss as a high profile, very successful psychiatrist who's always in control. He's written a book he feels extremely good about, called *Baby Steps.*

Bill Murray is a lovable neurotic who adores the book and attaches himself to the doctor and his family. Even when they go on vacation, he follows them. Dreyfuss can't stand having this manipulating intruder around and tries his best to get rid of him. But the family kind of likes this peculiar fellow named Bob, and eventually they become emotionally attached to him.

The film is appropriately called *What About Bob?* The bottom-line question is: What's to be done about this nutty guy?

When in ministry, encountering these "Bob" types is inevitable, so I could easily identify with what was happening in the script.

I first saw *"What About Bob?"* on a United flight and, in my laughter, it was everything I could do to keep from rolling in the aisle of the plane. Then I went to a theater and the content was even better and funnier the second time. When we watched it at home on video, I started laughing in anticipation as soon as the opening credits started rolling.

You see, Dreyfuss knows he needs a vacation, and he has to get this patient out of his life and out of his home or eventually Bob will destroy his well-ordered, overachieving, beautiful existence, which of course is exactly what happens.

Unable to work his way through this client/professional maze, in a complete reversal of roles, the psychiatrist is the one who ends up catatonic in a straight jacket in a mental hospital.

The film is on my top 20 list, and it's a comedy with profound implications. I won't read deeper thoughts into it than it deserves, except to say that a lot of times our mazes are complicated by other members of our family, or friends, or psychiatrists even, or ministers, or bosses, or

well-meaning neurotics; people over whom
we have no control. Problems don't usually
come in neat packages that can be worked
on one at a time. So in order to progress
from confusion to confidence, I've found it's
helpful to remove all unnecessary elements; to get rid of the Bobs, if you please,
when at all possible.

Jesus does this in Mark chapter 1 when
He tries to escape some of the pressures of
His work.

> *That evening after sunset the people
> brought to Jesus all the sick and
> demon-possessed. The whole town
> gathered at the door, and Jesus
> healed many who had various dis-
> eases. He also drove out many de-
> mons.... Very early in the morning,
> while it was still dark, Jesus got up,
> left the house and went off to a soli-
> tary place, where He prayed. Simon
> and his companions went to look for
> Him, and when they found Him, they
> exclaimed: "Everyone is looking for
> you!"* [This was sort of like saying,
> "Would you believe we've got a whole
> town of Bobs back there!"] *Jesus re-
> plied, "Let us go somewhere else—to
> the nearby villages—so I can preach
> there also. That is why I have come."*

So He traveled throughout Galilee, preaching in their synagogues and driving out demons (Mark 1:32-39).

What's unfolding here is the common problem of other people unwittingly trying to set our Lord's agenda. But He won't allow it. He knows that if He continues to heal people, pretty soon every sick man, woman, boy, and girl in the whole world will come to where He is. The agenda will only get heavier, not lighter. What's most important in the limited time Christ has is to fulfill His Father's desires, which at the moment meant more preaching about His kingship or the Kingdom of God.

I'm told it's a characteristic of our contemporary generation to be scheduled to death. We are discovering that overactivity is not necessarily commendable. Whether you're struggling to find the mind of the Lord or to work your way through a broken romance, give yourself a breather from taking on more than you can handle. There's no merit in trying to impress people by how much you've accomplished, or can't complete, or don't know how to refuse. Better uncomplicate your life as much as possible so you can concentrate on what is really important.

Before coming to The Chapel Ministries 19 years ago, I started an inner city church on the near west side of Chicago. The point where all the expressways come together is called the Circle Exchange. Here the University of Illinois established a commuter campus in the 1960's and named it Circle Campus after the intersection. It's also where we started a brand-new Evangelical Free Church in 1967 and called it Circle Church. We grew rapidly for an inner-city congregation, and we got publicity in a lot of places—including *Time* magazine. During those years, we first started taking people into our home...our personal what-about-Bobs, and there's seldom been a time since when someone hasn't lived with us.

This past year a young man from a ministry home who was severely depressed lived in our furnished basement. But I found it hard, when facing intense pressure and misunderstanding all day at the office, to come home and feel the distress of someone battling his own demons.

My wife and I talked this over and arranged for him to live elsewhere for a month. Why? Because he wasn't worthy of our help? Of course not! It was because we needed to reduce the number of stresses in our lives and focus on what was most important for us.

I would never demean food-service workers. They are some of the hardest workers in
the world! It's also true that a lot of eating
goes on in the Scriptures and in the
Church. Acts 6 is a setting where the cause
of Christ is growing rapidly, and anyone
trying to give leadership to a burgeoning
church knows that growth brings its own
immense stresses. Here the Grecian Jews
started complaining because the Hebraic
Jews' widows were getting all the attention
when food was distributed.

> *So the Twelve gathered all the disci-*
> *ples together and said, "It would not*
> *be right for us to neglect the ministry*
> *of the word of God in order to wait on*
> *tables* [to make sure the knife and
> spoon are on the right side of the
> plate and that the meals are served
> in a way that's aesthetically pleasing
> and that no one's being cheated pro-
> portionally]. *Brothers, choose seven*
> *men from among you.... We will turn*
> *this responsibility over to them and*
> *will give our attention to prayer and*
> *the ministry of the word"* (Acts 6:2-4).

What was the result? "So the word of
God spread. The number of disciples in Jerusalem increased rapidly, and a large
number of priests became obedient to the

faith" (Acts 6:7). The bottom line was this rapid growth in the dissemination of the gospel. If that stopped, the Twelve knew they had missed their primary calling.

When visiting overseas I often find that my brothers and sisters in the Lord have a better understanding of Kingdom matters than I do. I know that native missionaries in lands like India have fixed their sights on evangelism and church planting in the vast unreached areas of their country. When I remind them about caring for the sick and making sure fellow believers have adequate food, they say, "Amen."

But they also insist that the primary resources they have—whether that's people, funds, time, skills, or material goods—must be invested in priorities as established in Scripture. They suspect the Western Church has occupied many of its mission leaders and a vast amount of its resources in matters of food distribution—and on a scale far larger than in this passage—or in being unable to say *no* like Jesus did to the long lines of sick people. I, for one, am grateful for their insights and believe it's good to have my thinking challenged in this regard.

Wheel spinning is an indication that people wanting to go somewhere need help. They're in the unenviable position of trying to figure out what to do when they don't know what to do. The problem can be intensely personal, and might involve a given local church, a denomination, or the combined resources of a large united effort. A key principle I am learning that applies to this sort of situation is this: *To move from confusion to confidence, you must do your best to remove any of life's unnecessary elements.* That's something you can do when you don't know what to do.

Let me share two personal illustrations. Several weeks ago my daughter called with word that a friend was selling a well-trained yellow lab for a good price. They're great dogs. Our Old English sheepdog died five years ago, and I like the idea of a large dog around the house for Karen's protection since she works alone in her study so much. But as we talked, we both agreed that this wasn't the time to complicate our lives with a new animal. We're trying to cut back on responsibilities, not add more. That doesn't mean we'll never get a dog, but this just isn't the time. Again, it doesn't seem like a big thing, but it is a small complication that could expand to major proportions.

For the same reason, Karen has chosen to not travel in itinerant ministry for two years. She's completed her time as chair-person of the national board of InterVar-sity Christian Fellowship. Now she wants to carve out more time to be with the Lord, to slow things down personally in order to get a better handle on this whirligig we've been riding.

Hebrews 12:1-2 reads, "...let us throw off everything that hinders and the sin that so easily entangles, and let us run with perseverance the race marked out for us. Let us fix our eyes on Jesus, the author and perfecter of our faith, who for the joy set before Him endured the cross...."

Another recent film starting with the word *what* was the odd little study enti-tled, *What's Eating Gilbert Grape?* Johnny Depp plays a likable young character stuck in life with not much of a future. He's a small-town Iowa grocery clerk who stocks shelves and fills customers' orders. He also has two people he cares for, and he truly loves them both. One is a younger brother who's mentally retarded and has the bad habit of regularly climbing up the town wa-tertower and scaring the daylights out of everyone. The second person is Gilbert's mother, who must weigh at least 500 pounds and lives her entire life in the family house, which is falling to pieces around them.

Then a free-spirited and delightful young gal Gilbert's age comes through town. She's vacationing in a trailer with her grandmother. Thus the story line, with all these unusual characters, engenders tension between the young man's responsibility to his family and his desire to escape all this for his personal happiness. It's heartwarming and funny and melancholic all at the same time, probably very much like American small towns in the 1960's. With all these crazy situations I've mentioned, of course Depp's character has too many things he's juggling.

But then you also have to throw into the mix a lonely middle-aged married woman, his grocery store customer, who has been encouraging him to deliver her groceries and enticing him into the house with intentions that aren't honorable. Being in ministry, and seeing how these situations entrap so many people outside of celluloid life, I want to yell in the theater, "Get out of there, Gilbert. You don't need that complication too!"

I know my shouts of warning won't do any good because it's only a movie, and the film will go right on telling its story over and over regardless of a preacher's concerns. But the principle remains: It's not smart to drop sin into what is already a maze setting.

Dealing with sin while plodding through a labyrinth is akin to going to battle carrying two or three times the equipment you need. The enemy takes advantage of complicated situations to further entrap your life. Clearly, this is what the Depp story reveals: Sin increases pain, not pleasure.

We all have enough to handle just getting through life's complex situations. What we want to do is kick free of the confusions and move into confidence, and for that we all need the Lord's help. Unfortunately, "sin that entangles" only creates a distance between ourselves and the Lord. The writer of Hebrews reminds us that in our struggle against sin, we haven't yet reached the place where we've resisted to the point of shedding our blood like Jesus did (see Heb. 12:4).

But it's not just sexual sins we must flee.

> *Do not let any unwholesome talk come out of your mouths.... And do not grieve the Holy Spirit of God, with whom you were sealed for the day of redemption. Get rid of all bitterness, rage and anger, brawling*

and slander, along with every form of malice (Ephesians 4:29-31).

This passage reminds me of my favorite play. Last summer I saw for the third time a marvelous production of it performed at Stratford in Ontario, Canada, at the Shakespeare Festival. In every season, the company also mounts works by other playwrights. The play I love is Rostand's *Cyrano de Bergerac*; it's about a French swordsman who has a ridiculously large nose. What a complex and marvelous character he presents: a witty, brave braggadocio, as well as a romantic, true poet.

Perhaps you've seen the scene where Cyrano is helping a handsome musketeer, Christian, to court the beautiful Roxanne under her balcony. He's hidden from her sight by the night. Both love her, but Cyrano does so secretly. He feeds Christian his lines, but it's not working. Finally, in the darkness, Cyrano takes matters into his own hands, pushes Christian aside, and courts her for Christian with his own mouth and with his own loving words.

The theater-goer figures out long before the final scene that Roxanne probably doesn't really care what the one who was courting her looks like. She loves the *soul* of the person writing exquisite letters to her from the battlefield, signed "Christian" but composed by Cyrano. The story ends sadly and tragically with all suspecting that Cyrano and Roxanne could have made it. Of course they could have—except that the narrative is complicated by his anger and rage and brawling and pride. He has given the devil a foothold to mess up everything he holds dear in his life.

We must get rid of rage and anger, brawling, and every form of malice, as Paul wrote. "Do not give the devil a foothold," he warned in Ephesians 4:27.

As I implied earlier, I've known the what-about-Bobs; I've known the Gilbert Grapes and the Cyranos from towns other than Bergerac. Their stories, real stories, are too often bittersweet tales that become tragic because too many unnecessary complications ruined the promising future.

Another appropriate text to help us uncomplicate our struggles is this: "Therefore do not worry about tomorrow, for tomorrow will worry about itself." This is Jesus speaking, of course. "Each day has enough trouble of its own" (Mt. 6:34).

I'm told the younger generations have a lot of fears. That's not good. Most fears land on the side of confusion and complications. The opposite of fear is confidence and courage.

I am finding that while in a maze, there is a constant temptation to pick up next month's problems, mull over all the what-ifs, and try to figure them out. We're tempted to look at next week and ask, "If one of my key creditors really puts the squeeze on, will I have a game plan worked out? The day after tomorrow, when this board meeting takes place, what should my strategy be if this happens or that happens?" Those simple words of Christ have saved me from compulsive rumination. "This day has enough trouble of its own." It's like Jesus is telling us to live this one day and give Him time to answer our prayers and do some divine intervention work for the future.

You see, when I don't know what to do, one obvious thing I *can* do is pray.

> *Do not be anxious about anything, but in everything, by prayer and petition, with thanksgiving, present your requests to God. And the peace of God, which transcends all understanding, will guard your hearts and your minds in Christ Jesus* (Philippians 4:6-7).

Believe it or not!

The concept of not worrying about tomorrow is relatively new to me. But then I have to admit that it seems to be working, and obedience has not only saved me a lot of sweat, but also given me this strange sense of confidence that the Lord is going before me even as He promised He would (see Jn. 10:4).

So in this maze of frustration and confusion that is my life, I, David Mains, am fixing my eyes on Jesus, the pioneer and perfecter of my faith. He is the pioneer, the one who goes ahead and blazes a trail for others, as well as the perfecter, the mentor who brings maturity and strength to people like you and me who used to tremble in our spiritual trail boots. What about you? What are you fixing your eyes on? Complications? Clutter? Confusions? Or Christ?

Here I am, an outsider to the personal difficulties of others, admittedly not knowing all that much about the mazes you must traverse. Most likely, I come from a different world and different circumstance than yours. I feel a little like Jethro the priest back in Exodus 18, whom Moses had to accommodate because he was his father-in-law. The prophet had sent for his wife and two sons as he began a wilderness trek, and they couldn't really travel on their own. So Jethro escorted them to the camp of Israel.

Scripture reads that Jethro was delighted to hear all the good things the Lord had done and the daring deliverance of God's people from the Egyptians. Then Moses didn't have any time for Jethro anymore.

First thing the next day, Moses took his seat as judge. I would imagine they were tough cases, something like deciding whether O.J. Simpson was guilty of killing his wife and another man, or whether he was a victim of town gossip. Moses had who knows how many mind-boggling trials.

Dad-in-law Jethro sees the burden of Moses and exclaims, "What you are doing is not good. You need to get rid of all these extra elements in your life in order to do what is most important! You must be the people's representative before God. Get others to help bear your load. Stop trying to control all these many, many jobs. Delegation will make your load lighter." (See Exodus 18.)

What did Jethro know? He had only been there a day or two.

Hey, sometimes the outsider can see things better than the insider. What Jethro was saying to his famous son-in-law was that in order to progress from confusion to confidence, it is helpful, often even imperative, to rid yourself of all unnecessary distractions.

What's beautiful about Moses is that he listened to his father-in-law and did everything he said. The Bible records that from then on Moses was less burdened by the tasks he did not need to handle. Taking his father-in-law's advice helped him to be a better leader for the thousands who depended upon him to set the direction for the wilderness passage.

I hope some of you will heed my words to you as well.

What to Do

Here are some suggestions to help you live out what you've learned in this chapter.

1. Use the "off" button. Sometimes we're not even aware when the television competes with the task at hand. Get rid of distractions. Use a program listing to plan which programs you'll watch today, and when they're over, turn the television off. Cancel subscriptions to that magazine of decorating ideas—your list of things you'd like to do for your house is swamped under all the back issues anyway. Go ahead and listen to your music while you're preparing supper, but since you can't hear the CD player from your bedroom, why not give it a rest? Our brains can only take so much input; put in what's necessary and leave out what isn't.

2. Get off the spiritual treadmill. We all have many things we'd like to work on in our spiritual lives, but becoming a saint overnight is more than most of us can handle! God doesn't expect you to be a spiritual giant; He expects you to mature as His child. Find just one goal you feel your Father would want you to work toward. It may be to have more of

a servant's attitude, or to reserve 15 minutes each day for your Adventure Journal. Work on that one discipline until you know it's become a good, solid habit; then move on to something else. Remember, the 50-Day Adventure is intended to be "guilt free." You have your whole life to grow in the Lord—keep yourself in shape, but don't kill your spirit.

3. Just say *no*. For many of us, that's a hard word to say. When someone asks us to do something, we might think "the Christian thing" is to fit it in somehow. However, you don't have to do everything; you have to do what God calls you to do. If the pastor's wife asks you to teach Sunday school because you're such a good deacon and everyone respects you in your Tuesday night Bible study, explain to her (kindly, please) that you wouldn't be a good deacon or Bible study leader if you were teaching Sunday school as well. Don't take on more than you can handle, or else you won't be effective at what you *could* have handled.

4. Take one step at a time. You don't have to clean the whole house, organize your entire garage, and totally revamp your

workspace this week. Start with one thing—a closet, a desk drawer, one corner of the memo board—and work through that. When you've finished with one, pat yourself on the back, give yourself a little rest, and move on to something else. Before you know it, you'll have done far more than you expected.

5. Accept your weight. That's a shocking statement, isn't it? Everything in our culture says, "Be skinny. Try to wear the clothes you wore in college. That's healthy." Losing weight may or may not be healthy for you, but the pressure of fitting into those clothes probably isn't. Are the things you've outgrown taking needed space at the back of your closet, or filling boxes among the Christmas decorations in your attic? True, you may fit in them again someday, but right now they're cluttering your life. Besides, you have enough to worry about without adding a diet to the list. So keep one favorite shirt or skirt as an incentive or a humorous reminder, then give the rest to someone with growing kids, or to a young friend who is the size you were back then (and don't be jealous—weight comes with age). Of course, you can always take clothes to the Salvation Army or ask your local veterans society to

pick them up. Then when you *do* lose those extra pounds, it'll be a great reward to go out and buy some new outfits.

6. Imagine yourself on your deathbed. That shouldn't be too depressing, as long as you're paying attention to what's most important. If you were dying, you probably wouldn't say, "I wish I'd kept the house cleaner," or "I wish I'd spent more time at the business." What *would* you say? Spend a few minutes pondering what's most essential in life, and write down three of your conclusions in your Bible or a journal. Concentrate on changing your habits in at least one of those areas so you can be pleased when you look back on your life.

Especially for Families

7. Hold a garage sale. Take a family weekend to go through the clutter in your house. Do you have jewelry you never wear, games the kids are too old for, and tools you don't use piled in the back of the basement? Let your children volunteer items to sell; have them clean out their rooms and their toy boxes. Make a few "garage sale" signs out of the extra poster board left from your sixth grader's science project, and sell all those things that get in your way. If the

kids are old enough, have them take charge of your garage sale—they'll find it great fun, while you'll have a chance to teach them about making change and the value of money. Then use whatever you make for a family outing, or ask your children if they know of anyone who might benefit from it. Let them have the pleasure of taking what they've earned and giving it in the name of the Lord.

8. Get used to delegating. Meet as a family and ask your children to participate in all the work of running the household. Have the kids "donate" specific tasks— they'll be more likely to do something they've volunteered for! Let Susie make dinner once a week (even if you have to supervise the first few times, she'll be able to do it herself someday). Put Jody in charge of making up a shopping list. See if Nathan can rock the baby to sleep each evening. Ask your spouse to help you with ironing the clothes or figuring out the finances. As long as you're cheerful about it, your family members will assure you that they'd rather help you than see you flustered and irritable because you can't do it all yourself.

Chapter 6

God's Grace and Forgiveness

A good maze is not designed to be solved quickly. If there's no challenge to it, then it probably should be called something else— a strolling garden, for instance. The word *maze* implies a certain degree of difficulty.

But what would you think of a misconstrued maze that has no exit route? The workman who built the walls, or the gardener who planted the hedges, or the graphic artist who designed the puzzle made a mistake and every escape was blocked! Some of the labyrinths in which we find ourselves feel as though they were constructed by a cruel or sadistic architect.

I should have mentioned this before, but it's a mistake to assume that all of life's mazes follow certain rules. Because of human error, a great number of tragedies can occur in mazes. It would be naive not to remind yourself about the risks of meandering on your own through these complexities.

I frequently think that my adult children have inherited a world that's not as good as the one to which I was introduced six decades ago. Did you know that the experts sometimes refer to today's young adults as the Repair Generation? This is because of the economic, environmental, and family-of-man messes they're going to have to clean up. It reminds me of one particular scene in the film *Jurassic Park*, where there's a shot of what looks like a small mountain of dinosaur poop. It seems as if this generation has been given a shovel and told that its job is to clean up these colossal mounds that appear just about everywhere on the landscape.

Yes, it's a messed-up world, and we're all messed-up people who do some good, but who can't seem to stop doing a lot of bad too. Our best efforts come apart far quicker than we want. Our moments to remember are like the brief shining one that was known as Camelot, which even the best of the best messed-up: Arthur, Guinevere, and Lancelot.

People make a lot of mistakes. They over-schedule their lives. They fall into sexual sin. They get angry. They sink into depression. They abuse their spouses. They literally try to vanish by not eating. They get confused about their gender. They gamble. They cheat. They kill. Put messed-up people in a messed-up-world maze, and you should expect to end up with mountains of trouble.

That's why I quickly add that messed-up people in a messed-up world would do well to accept the Lord's grace and forgiveness. We all need to get used to drawing on this boundless source because, regardless of whose fault it is, sooner or later we all will run smack into a wall, or get trapped down some no-exit corridor. Maybe the dead end wasn't there the last time you negotiated that passage, so you thought you could run a fast track. But it was there this time! You forgot that mazes don't have agreed-upon rules.

So where does this leave you?

*****

Sorry, with all the grunting around here I didn't hear you. No, no, I know your story. Yeah, the big bucks from Dad and how they bought you friends and fun and wouldn't it be great if life could remain like that forever, and—what was the license plate on the truck that hit you? Talk louder please, those pigs are noisy when they eat.

So you think you'll go home, is that your plan? Admit you were a fool, ask to work somewhere in the family business 'cause any lowly, menial task would be better than this degrading hovel? How do you think your dad will respond? You blew a lot of his bucks, you know. He's liable to punch your lights out. Going home might be a stupid idea.

So he got up and went to his father. But while he was still a long way off, his father saw him and was filled with compassion for him; he ran to his son, threw his arms around him and kissed him. The son said to him, "Father, I have sinned against heaven and against you. I am no longer worthy to be called your son." But the father said to his servants, "Quick! Bring the best robe and put it on him. Put a ring on his finger and sandals on his feet. Bring the fattened calf and kill it. Let's have a feast and celebrate. For this son of mine was dead and is alive again; he was lost and is found"... (Luke 15:20-24).

*****

This story is a powerful picture of the grace and forgiveness that has been memorialized in sermons and in people's lives

down through the centuries ever since
Christ first told it. Its truth has to sound as
good in your ears as it does in mine. We can't
earn this grace, but we certainly need it.

We especially need grace and forgiveness when we feel trapped in a maze, for
when we're not used to the frustrations of
these confinements, we say things we
shouldn't. We also think things we
shouldn't, we do things we shouldn't, and
too often we mess up in ways we shouldn't!

Maybe we need to be told how bad we
are (but maybe we already know that), and
maybe most of all we need to be repeatedly
reminded about God's incredible grace and
forgiveness.

Have you seen the film *Little Women*?
Men, it's a good movie; you ought to see it.
For a change it's about a healthy and lov-
ing family.

Laurie is the fellow who's a long-time
family friend, the rich boy next door, and
he loves Jo, one of the four March daughters. Jo is beautifully played by the actress
Winona Ryder in the 1995 remake. In one
touching scene, Laurie returns from college where he's been a bit of a prodigal. But
he's always loved Jo and he attempts to
propose to her by the old fence in the
meadow. She tries like everything to side-
track him: "Please don't do this. It would
never work. We'd kill each other."

"If you loved me, Jo," he says, "I should be a perfect saint, for you could make me anything you like."

"I'm sorry, I just can't. Let's keep it as best of friends, which we are." She's most uncomfortable.

Now he's mad! "You'll be sorry someday!" And he storms off.

"Where are you going?" she asks, as his face frightens her.

In the book by Louisa May Alcott, his response is, "To the devil," and for some months that's where he goes. The handsome, attractive, wealthy Laurie has just hit a wall flush on! This is a humiliating, devastating, traumatizing rejection for the young man.

If in the film he had said, "Okay, let's remain friends like you suggested. In time I'll be all right," he wouldn't have felt the welter of emotions some people experience when they've been told they're not loved. When that happens, men and women don't always act like perfect saints. This deeply disturbing rejection causes the world to tilt. Then, by an overtly negative reaction of grief or rage, they are capable of making matters even worse. Much, much worse. But hear me— *it is not so much worse that what they do is beyond God's grace and forgiveness.*

Laurie eventually straightens out and, would you believe, he falls in love with and marries Amy, the youngest of the sisters. He turns out to be a fine man, and it is a fine match.

Would you also believe that lots of disappointed people—many losers, repeated failures, even broken folk—discover marvelous futures? They become whole and grateful adults. Somewhere along the line, they learn about the miracle of grace and forgiveness.

This is not a matter of their earning their way back. Grace is more than making up for the bad with great efforts at good. Grace is given freely and must be accepted freely. That's why we call it the Father's amazing grace.

(I know I'm referring to movies quite often, but in this visual culture, these fresh film pictures sometimes clarify the points a minister struggles to illustrate.)

In 1986 a film was produced by the same people who did *The Killing Fields* and *Chariots of Fire*. It starred Jeremy Irons and Robert DeNiro and was called *The Mission*. Irons plays Father Gabriel, a Spanish Jesuit, who goes to the eighteenth century South American wilderness to build a mission in hopes of converting the

Indians. Actor Robert DeNiro plays Mendoza, a slave hunter/profiteer who plundered the same people. In a fit of jealous rage over a woman, Mendoza kills his brother, and is overwhelmed with grief and guilt for what he's done.

Wanting to aid the process of repentance, the Jesuits devise a means of penance whereby Mendoza lugs an impossibly heavy load up the side of a steep cliff. It's a long and tortuous scene as he tugs and scrambles to get this huge net filled with the armor he used to capture slaves to the top. Finally, he reaches the summit where, totally exhausted, he's met by Indians who recognize him, their former enemy. In a new act of Christian love, they cut him free of his burden, which rolls and tumbles down the route he's just clambered up with incredible tenacity and sheer willpower. Literally and emotionally, Mendoza is suddenly released, and he cries and laughs and cries and laughs some more. It is a classic film picture that graphically records the results of forgiveness.

Grace is not about carrying the impossible load up the side of your chosen cliff. It's about being set free by an act of divine love even though you're undeserving.

Some have yet to experience that marvelous gift. You're not a slave trader like

Mendoza, but you've been sleeping around with someone outside of marriage. You've cheated on taxes, reports, or tests. You're captive to an addiction of one kind or another. You're a rebel, but just why you are doesn't make as much sense to you as it once did. Maybe you're HIV positive, but nobody close to you knows you're carrying that burden in your net. Or you've denied your Lord, said to peers or to complete strangers in one way or another, "I'm not a Christian," even though Jesus has been incredibly gracious to you. Now, like Peter, or Mary Magdalene, or the slave trader-turned-hymn writer, John Newton, you need the Lord to put a new song in your heart about a marvelous sweet sound of amazing grace. You're the wayward daughter or son who needs to be found, the blind one feeling sorry for yourself who needs to be able to see again.

Through many mazes, toils, and snares, you have already come. If you've gotten free of them, I'm sure it's been grace that brought you safe thus far, and that will lead you home, for messed-up people in a messed-up world do well to accept the Lord's grace and forgiveness.

I hope that sounds good to you. It does to me!

I'm always touched when my close friend Dr. K.P. Yohannan, president of Gospel for Asia, tells about getting lost in the great American maze. Born in South India, he never wore shoes until his later teen years. Then as a young man, he was profoundly moved by a message given by George Verwer of Operation Mobilization. Deeply challenged about the purpose of his life, before long K.P. was involved with an evangelism team witnessing in North India. In this setting he experienced the paradox of hardship and joy, of having little but considering himself the most fortunate of people. Here was a cause worth living for, a calling that made the resistance of the crowds and the cat calls and the rocks aimed at him a privilege to face.

In time, he decided to come to the States for further training at a Bible school. The studies went well, but that's not all K.P. learned about in this seductive land. Like the brother of the prodigal in Luke 15, his heart started to lose the warmth of his Father's love for lost children. What began to concern him was whether God was giving him all that was his by rights.

In his book, *Revolution in World Missions*, K.P. writes:

"From the moment I touched foot on American soil, I walked in an unbelieving daze. How can two so different economies co-exist simultaneously on the earth? Everything was overpowering and confusing to me."

The story continues in his second book, *The Road to Reality*:

"I was preaching, studying the Word for hours daily and shepherding a flock of 200 souls. Our church was growing. The congregation was being fed the Word of God. People were being saved, but I was miserable inside.

"My soul was drying up. I was tormented by the knowledge I carried about inside my heart and head. Others had not seen what I had seen in Asia, and I could not forget the people I had left behind. I was haunted by memories of millions of lost souls in North India, and the suffering, forgotten little band of native missionaries I knew was still trying to reach them for God.

"So for two years, my heart had hardened. I had not shed a tear for them. In fact, I could not shed a tear for anyone or anything. Then, as I prayed and evaluated my life in the light of eternity, it all changed. I let go of one materialistic thing after another—to surrender my ambitions and plans for future ministry in the safety and security of America.

"Our life-style became simpler. My new car was the first thing to go. Insurance policies, saving accounts, credit cards, most of my clothes— everything that could be was sold off so the money could be sent to needy native brethren.

"But we never missed a thing. It was such a joy to move in the flow of the Holy Spirit again. Suddenly we were free. We had wings like eagles to soar above our bondage to these material playthings. In one stroke, we as a family were again having a significant impact on a lost and dying world. We knew that we were exercising the mind of Christ about these things, and we began trusting our Father to provide for our needs."

K.P. Yohannan is not the only person who has performed better under hardship than in the maze of blessing. Even so, the

Lord extended grace and forgiveness toward him and gave him a powerful ministry. Here are similar words of testimony from the pen of the Psalmist David, another leader who did better in fire than he did in favor:

> *The Lord is compassionate and gracious, slow to anger, abounding in love. He will not always accuse, nor will He harbor His anger forever; He does not treat us as our sins deserve or repay us according to our iniquities. For as high as the heavens are above the earth, so great is His love for those who fear Him; as far as the east is from the west, so far has He removed our transgressions from us. As a father has compassion on his children, so the Lord has compassion on those who fear Him; for He knows how we are formed, He remembers that we are dust* (Psalm 103:8-14).

As people of dust, we must not mistake being a Christian with never falling short of God's expectations, or those of our spouse or friends. Following Jesus doesn't mean you don't get so frustrated with life that you suddenly shock everyone, including yourself, with an expletive, or a string of them. Being saved doesn't insure that your business will succeed or that a trusted employee won't secretly rob you blind. Christian couples who sacrifice so their sons or daughters can attend Christian schools have no guarantees how they will turn out. The Church is a true sanctuary or safe place, but as a refuge or haven it still isn't free from the troubles that the rest of society knows all too well. Everyone in the family of God isn't perfect and problem-free. The truth is that nobody is, including the most respected of church leaders. Yes, we know the broad path leads to destruction, but sometimes the narrow path seems to have "pit stops" there too.

Hey, wherever the less-than-best place you're in is, I don't want you to think, "I've blown it, and though in a way I'd like to go back to my spiritual roots, if my Father in Heaven is anything like I picture He should be, He'll punch my lights out."

If you think that, then you've got the wrong picture of Him in your head. The devil's put a horror-picture poster in the theater window when, in reality, what's playing is a tender love story, a divine romance.

- It's a picture about knowing Camelot again.

- It's a tale about a theme park of a much earlier time—not Jurassic Park, but Eden restored.
- It's the real report of an amazing God who frees people of the crushing burdens they try to carry up steep cliffs.
- It's a "happy ending" story of a prodigal who went to the devil, but came back home to be surprised by a love that changed him forever.
- It's a narrative account of a Christian worker from India who got mixed up trying to negotiate an American maze, but now in the Lord's great mercy is helping others see clearly through their own puzzles.
- It's a true-to-life plot that we've all been thrust into, about left turns, right turns, dead ends, and an unimaginable God who is pointing us down the right path.
- It's the Author of Life's portrayal of a direction for tomorrow's maze, and it's His promise of eventual freedom from this difficult terrain.

It's a blockbuster story you don't want to miss, especially if yours is one of the starring roles.

What to Do

Here are some suggestions to help you live out what you've learned in this chapter.

1. Add and subtract a weight. When trying to learn a spiritual or emotional lesson, it's sometimes helpful to use a physical analogy. The example of Mendoza's penance in *The Mission* (see p. 120 of this chapter), is a powerful illustration of an attempt to get rid of sin's heaviness. Try wearing a backpack full of heavy books one day. Put a few rocks in your purse, or add something heavy to a chain you usually wear around your neck. Take a minute every so often to feel the weight of whatever you're carrying. It's uncomfortable, isn't it? Ask a friend to take that weight off you at the end of the day, and notice how much more free you feel. Then remember that the freedom God's grace and forgiveness bring you is far greater than this physical example can possibly demonstrate.

2. Read John Bunyan's *Pilgrim's Progress*. If you can't take time for the whole book, read Part One through Christian's struggle with his burden and his encounter at the foot of the cross. If you

were to describe your own experience at the foot of the cross, what would you say? Tell someone your story, remembering that God's grace and forgiveness are available for all of our "burdens," as long as we come to the cross in repentance.

3. Play the spy. Watch how people around you—in your workplace, at your social hang outs, in your church—react to guilt. Does one of your friends say "I'm sorry" for *everything*? Do people seem relieved or incredulous when you pardon them for insulting you? Let it be your secret project to hunt out individuals who show signs of shame and extend forgiveness to them. Then remember this: God takes even more pleasure in being gracious to you, His child, than you do in forgiving mere acquaintances.

4. Study the "Restoration Chapters"—Jeremiah 31–33. These chapters describe how, after God vows to pour out His wrath on the wicked nation of Israel, He promises to bring them back to a favorable relationship with Him. We can and should take these words to heart for our own circumstances. God judges us, but more than anything else,

He wants us to be restored to Him. Take several days to let the thoughts in these chapters sink into your mind. Make them personal, for God is speaking directly to you: "...For I will forgive [your] wickedness and will remember [your] sins no more" (Jer. 31:34).

Especially for Families

5. Do your own drama. Act out the Prodigal Son story with your kids. The late Keith Green recorded an excellent song you can use as an outline for your skit. Or, for a shorter version, try miming to Benny Hester's "When God Ran" or some other suitable piece. Give each of your children a part—as a son, a servant, a partier, or even one of the pigs—and include their friends too, if you can. Do a Sunday night presentation for your church, or schedule a family performance to tell the story to grandparents or to your study group.

6. Note the way things heal. When your child cuts him or herself, you can actually use it as an opportunity to explore forgiveness! As you're putting a disinfectant on Anna's skinned knee, explain, "This is what the Holy Spirit does when we come to God all broken up and

dirty with sin. He makes us all clean so we can heal more quickly." If her older brother has an infection (or you could find a picture of an infection in an encyclopedia), you might use that as an example of not going to God. "When we don't come to God for forgiveness, our sins fester—they get worse and worse, uglier and uglier, until we think they may never heal." Encourage your little ones to run to God every time they sin, just as they run to you when they get hurt.

7. Play the "Grace Game." Pass out three-by-five cards at the dinner table or during your family devotion time. Have each person write down something he or she would like to have forgiven (or ask younger children to tell you what they'd like written for them). Present your cards to the Lord and to each other, asking for forgiveness. Then rip those cards up and throw them away to symbolize what God does for us. This can be a particularly meaningful time if requests are directed toward specific people. For instance, if you need to be forgiven for needlessly nagging your teenager, ask her to rip up the card for you. If those mistakes you each have made resurface during the next few

days (Cathi teases you *again* about eating the Twinkie she was saving for her brown-bag lunch), remind each other of how God has forgiven you. Just make sure you don't take that forgiveness as an excuse to make more mistakes.

8. Be a healthy model of God. Your children's concept of God their Father will be partially a result of your actions as a parent. Scary, isn't it? But you can have a wonderful influence on kids by teaching them how to handle sin. If you must punish them, sit them down and explain that the punishment is a consequence of what they've done wrong. If they ask you for forgiveness, they may still have to bear the punishment (or they may not, if you feel you can be merciful!), but you will always love them. Give them plenty of hugs, and make sure you don't act angry with them after they've asked for pardon. Your little tyke's reaction to his guilt, and his relief when he understands that you still love him, may hold a lesson about the Lord for you too.

Chapter 7

Jesus Struggled Too

The subtitle for the movie *Apollo 13* could easily have been "What to Do When You Don't Know What to Do." You probably remember the poster: Tom Hanks, playing Jim Lovell, peers back at you over the shoulder of his astronaut garb. His eyes are wide; his face shows stress. Printed across the foot of the picture are the haunting words, "Houston, we have a problem."

Did they ever! In fact, as the head of the three-man crew, Lovell faced a host of problems. The flight date had been moved forward, so they had less time than planned to go through the rigorous training necessary for a lunar mission. Not long before their launching day, NASA's flight surgeon determined that one crew member, Ken Mattingly, had been exposed to the measles and would almost certainly break out in them during the expedition.

So alternate Jack Swigert replaced him in the last few days of training. Then—on the way to the moon, during a routine stirring of the oxygen tanks—part of Lovell's service module exploded.

Suddenly the Apollo 13 is venting oxygen. The crew has to shut down the command module and enter the adjoining lunar-landing ship as a temporary safe haven. In the part of outer space where they are, the temperature can fall as low as 280 degrees below zero. Even so, the lunar module is powered down to conserve what now is a very limited amount of energy—which leaves the crew in a cold predicament.

As time passes, the outlook gets pretty grim. The astronauts are bone tired and freezing. One of them, Fred Haisy, has a fever. As if that's not enough, an alarm sounds a warning that the deadly carbon dioxide level has risen. It seems the moon-landing module was only designed to filter the carbon dioxide exhaled by two men for 36 hours; these three men have been in it for over 24 hours, and the filters are clogging. There are extra filters in the command module, but they're square-shaped and won't fit the round holes of the lunar module system.

Back in Houston, the missions control people stay up all night frantically trying to solve this square-peg-in-a-round-hole problem. Eventually they come up with what I would call a Rube Goldberg, or incredibly convoluted, way of making things work. Using tape, socks, food bags, cardboard, hoses, and whatever else they know is on the spaceship, they put together a system that can be duplicated by the crew of Apollo 13. And wonder of wonders, the makeshift adapter gets the job done!

Unfortunately, it's not long before another dilemma must be resolved. When the astronauts reenter the command module, which hopefully will bring them back to the earth, they aren't sure it can be powered up again.

It turns out that Ken Mattingly doesn't have the measles. That is fortunate because he knows this specific piece of equipment better than anyone else. As he climbs into the simulator at mission control in Houston he says, "I need this to be cold and dark. Give me the same conditions the men up there are facing."

After hours of work and several failed attempts, Mattingly comes up with the solution to maximizing the limited power available. In one of the most dramatic moments in the film, he gives his instructions to Swigert, the astronaut who replaced him on the mission. Jack carefully writes down Ken's instructions. Now everything rides on whether the dead command module can be brought back to life.

It's time to find out, but Swigert is exhausted. He has been on the spacecraft almost a week and hasn't had much sleep. He's nervous that things won't go right and, of course, it's bitterly cold. If there's even one loose seam that water has leaked into, the entire electrical system can short out and be destroyed. As he goes about his risky and lonely task, he mutters to himself, "This is like driving a toaster through a car wash."

"I'm having trouble reading my own writing," he falters. "There's an awful lot of condensation on the panels." Then this marvelous line comes from Ken Mattingly back in Houston. When I watched the film, it was like it leaped from the screen. "Don't worry about it," he tells Jack. "I'll talk you through it. Turn breaker 5 on...." The calm voice from Houston leads this nervous replacement astronaut through the proper sequence—and the command module starts.

Maybe seven chapters into this book you still see yourself in a particularly tough situation. Your given "toaster in a car wash" dilemma hasn't had time to work itself out, so you still don't know whether your systems will short out. When you try to explain to others what's happening and why you are particularly distressed, their eyes start to glaze over. Obviously they have trouble understanding. Their suggestions reveal that your friends haven't a clue about what's really going on. They couldn't be more out of it than if you were an Apollo 13 astronaut asking for help with your command module. So face it, your maze is unique and you shouldn't expect someone to be around who can talk you through it. Right?

Wrong!

One of the great discoveries about being a Christian is that Jesus can identify completely with our unique troubles. He's like a better-trained backup who has purposely put Himself in our predicaments, and is therefore more than qualified to talk us through these problems.

Maybe to you that thought reads like more "preacher words." "It's interesting sermon filler, but it's not much value in alleviating the pinch I feel in this tight spot." If that's what you're thinking, it's time for you to grasp my next suggestion for what to do when you don't know what to do: *Make your "maze time" an occasion to discover how much Jesus identifies with your struggles, and let Him be the one to talk you through what needs to be done.*

What if you're a single mom who doesn't have enough time in a day to do everything that needs to be done? You lack money to hire help, and people of the church are slow in lending a hand the way you would like. "Jesus, can You identify with what I'm going through?" you ask prayerfully. "I know You understand singleness, but did You ever have to get done in a day way more than what should be expected of one person?"

The answer, of course, is yes. Check out Christ's schedule in passages like Matthew 8 and 9. Few people squeezed as much into a day as our Lord did. Also note that after this extended time of preaching and healing He told His disciples, "The harvest is plentiful but the workers are few." Apparently He felt it would be nice to have more help.

Say you're an executive in a highly competitive field, and one or two bad decisions have put your entire corporation in jeopardy. Key employees are beginning to look for other challenges, and sometimes you almost wish you had that same option.

I can identify with you. Maybe that's why I liked Apollo 13 so much. It looked like there was no possible way there could be a successful conclusion to this troubled mission, yet somehow they pulled it off. I left the theater with hope.

"Come on, David," you respond. "Everybody thinks of you as a minister or a preacher, not a business executive."

Well, Jesus certainly knows what it's like filling the preacher role. But these days I'm reminding Him that I'm also the executive director of a 56-year-old, not-for-profit media corporation that employs about 45 people who may very well feel their jobs are at risk.

Each year one of our major assignments from the Lord is to organize a 50-Day Spiritual Adventure. The goal is to have one million North American participants in this time of accelerated spiritual growth called, this year, "What to Do When You Don't Know What to Do." Another million are expected to be involved throughout Asia, especially in India and Nepal.

To launch an Adventure requires a substantial amount of up-front money. For example, just the initial print-run of the English journals costs over $100,000. We also have to pay for 140—from October through January—Pastor and Church Leaders Conferences, which train those who will lead the Adventure in the estimated 8,000 participating churches. So there are airplane tickets to buy, Leader Manuals to print, videos to produce, test programs to run, and supplementary books to stock.

Most of the money that churches pay for their materials will not get to us until just before the Adventure begins. Another large number of church invoices will be paid following the actual 50 days of the Adventure. So how do I satisfy printers, travel agents, the Federal Express people, and a host of other suppliers by the 30-day grace period they extend when they initially send me their bills? Already my organization is strapped financially. Can Jesus identify with that kind of pressure?

I can almost hear the Lord say, "Yes, David, I can. I had a dream of a Kingdom that would be worldwide. Most of the people who first heard what I said didn't have the faintest idea how large that world is and what resources it would take to pull off what I had in mind. As I spoke, I had to keep on the move because Roman soldiers and jealous religious leaders were among those listening in the crowds. So I know what juggling is all about! Wondering whether key people will stick with you when the going gets tough...believe Me, I can identify with that."

It's amazing to me how well Christ can identify with most of our mazes, in spite of the fact that His life here was quite short. He knows what it's like to grow up in a setting where people questioned His dreams rather than believing in them. He understands how it feels not to be attractive, to be despised and rejected, and even to be looked upon as a sinner.

Long before our Lord made His appearance on earth, the prophet Isaiah wrote these words about Christ:

> ...*He had no beauty or majesty to attract us to Him, nothing in His appearance that we should desire Him. He was despised and rejected by men, a man of sorrows, and familiar with suffering...* (Isaiah 53:2-3).

So many brothers and sisters in Third World countries have told me about the physical violence they have suffered because of their witness for Christ. When a conversation like this takes place, I find myself being very quiet. I know nothing about such experiences. I never had tomatoes or eggs thrown at me, much less stones. No one has ever heckled me when I preached. But these men and women know what it means to stand in the face of adversity and talk of their love for Jesus and what He can do for a life. They are the ones who have represented their Lord's alternative kingship in areas where people have never before heard Jesus' name. Often their boldness puts into motion the clash of the kingdoms of light and darkness.

Though I have trouble understanding their experiences, I am so grateful that Christ is familiar with suffering. He can say to these people, "I know what it's like to be spit upon, to have My beard yanked from My face, to have My back lashed raw, to be nailed to a cross, to be hung naked before an angry crowd, and to hear them heckle Me. I've been there. I can talk you through that awful maze."

The writer to the Hebrews states in chapter 2, verse 18: "Because He Himself suffered when He was tempted, He is able to help those who are being tempted." Two chapters later, Hebrews 4:15-16 reads:

> *For we do not have a high priest who is unable to sympathize with our weaknesses, but we have one who has been tempted in every way, just as we are—yet was without sin. Let us then approach the throne of grace with confidence, so that we may receive mercy and find grace to help us in our time of need.*

Finding "grace to help us in our time of need" sounds to me like making our time in a maze an occasion for discovering how much Jesus identifies with our struggles, and then letting Him talk us through what needs to be done.

Jesus' identifying with what we're going through doesn't necessarily mean that any of us can understand what He experienced. Like the old African-American spiritual says, "Jesus walked this lonesome valley, He had to walk it all alone. Nobody else could walk it for Him." In Philippians Paul writes about the God/man in chapter 2:

And being found in appearance as a man, He humbled Himself and be-came obedient to death—even death on a cross! Therefore God exalted Him to the highest place and gave Him the name that is above every name, that at the name of Jesus every knee should bow, in heaven and on earth and under the earth, and every tongue confess that Jesus Christ is Lord, to the glory of God the Father (Philippians 2:8-11).

Realizing His uniqueness, I'm quick to say, "Lord, who do I know like You? Yes, You can identify with what I'm going through because You lived on this earth as

I do. But You're also the marvelous Son of God who honors me greatly by offering Your help. I'm listening—please talk me through what needs to be done."

Sometimes I pray those words before going to the Scriptures. Then certain verses will stand out as I read them. On other occasions I'll be in a prayerful frame of mind while driving, and the Lord will remind me of wonderful promises He made when here on earth.

In my current situation, He has repeatedly taken me back to the Sermon on the Mount and talked about the lilies of the field not laboring or spinning, while King Solomon in all his wonder was not dressed as well as they were. So why should I worry about things like clothes, food, shelter, or future 50-Day Adventure concerns? My Lord's specific words are: "Therefore do not worry about tomorrow [David], for tomorrow will worry about itself. Each day has enough trouble of its own" (Mt. 6:34).

Maybe the Lord wants to say to you, "Are not two sparrows sold for a penny? Yet not one of them will fall to the ground apart from the will of your Father. ... So don't be afraid; you are worth more than many sparrows" (Mt. 10:29,31). Or, "You have heard that it was said, 'Love your neighbor and hate your enemy.' But I tell you: Love your enemies and pray for those who persecute you" (Mt. 5:43-44). It could be a word about not storing up for yourself treasures on earth, where they'll likely be destroyed or stolen someday. Jesus may be telling you to make sure your treasure is in Heaven, where it will be safe and indestructible: "For where your treasure is, there will your heart be also" (Mt. 6:21). It's not Houston, but Heaven that reminds you, "I am the true vine, and My Father is the gardener. He cuts off every branch in Me that bears no fruit, while every branch that does bear fruit He prunes [trims clean] so that it will be even more fruitful" (Jn. 15:1-2).

My personal conviction is that Christ always has special words He wants to impress on your mind during stress-filled times. Most often they will be gentle and kind—words from someone who is fully aware of the pressures you're going through. He understands the multiplicity of those space shuttle-type problems that come one after another, but He promises to talk you through them. You will not be destroyed. This confusing maze will be mastered if you follow His instructions.

I find journaling to be an integral part of this process. It's important that you put on paper what Jesus has impressed on your heart and how His thoughts give direction and meaning to your life. Notes taken during the journey are what can later transform a maze experience into a good story.

You see, all good scripts are built on conflict. Without conflict, there's really not much of a story to tell. A conflict that takes a turn for the worse is called a tragedy. What you want is an *Apollo 13* type of ending. Granted, no one on that mission got to walk on the moon. But it was still a victory of sorts. There remained valid reasons for rejoicing. It certainly was a phenomenal story to tell!

I have a hunch that one of the great pastimes in eternity will be watching people's stories that were never appreciated on earth the way they should have been. Some of you reading this chapter may be heroes in accounts that will be favorites of the world yet to come. My guess is that certain of you, who often feel bone tired and alone yet keep on following what Jesus tells you, will be the ones most applauded in the future life.

Jim Lovell is an unusual person. His saga was retold while he was still alive. He's become a hero because a film was made about what took place on his mission. But in eternity, there will be more than enough time to see to it that all good stories are appreciated. And I have a feeling that in each of them there will be a particularly moving scene where the One who now often plays a backup role and allows us to appear as stars says, "Don't worry about it, Jack" (or Karen or David or Margaret or Thomas or Luciana, or whomever); "I've got this thing figured out. If you listen to Me, everything will turn out fine. Now, let Me talk you through it."

What to Do

Here are some suggestions to help you live out what you've learned in this chapter.

1. Go to the Gospels. Read through the story of Jesus' life and make a note of any time He might have felt disappointed, hurt, or unhappy. His disciples often didn't have a clue who He was or what was happening right in front of them; the religious leaders of the day were totally against Him. A close friend betrayed Him, and one of His best friends disowned Him when He was going through the hardest time of His life. How were the Lord's situations similar to your own?

2. Dig into the account of the Temptation. Examine what happened when Jesus encountered satan in the wilderness (see Mt. 4:1-11), and keep that account in mind as you go through your day. How were the struggles He faced similar to your own? What did He do to overcome them? Each time you wish you could eat a lot, or would like to appear especially important, or want to do something dynamic to impress those around you (or anything else that applies), think back to Jesus' answers to

these temptations. Then pray that
Christ will give you His strength to face
your own wildernesses. Rely on Him to
help you in your struggle; He's been
through it already.

3. Watch the news broadcast. Things are
happening throughout the world today
that must disappoint God. People mis-
treat the environment; wars break out
that kill hundreds of thousands; atheis-
tic attitudes counter every moral foundation He set up. How might these
affect the Lord the way your maze af-
fects you?

4. Let yourself daydream. Picture yourself
with Jesus on one of the days recorded
in the Gospels. Imagine what He looked
like and how He sounded. What happened during the course of your day together? The Gospel of Luke has some
good specifics. What did He say when
He was tired, annoyed, delighted, or excited? How did Jesus' humanness show
itself? How was He different from you,
and how was He similar? Do you imagine Him encountering any confusing
maze-times? How did He find His way?
Perhaps much of the daydream will be
conjecture; remember, we can't take our

conceptions as fact. But we can hold on to the truth that Christ went through what we go through. He understands what it's like to be human.

5. Read *In His Steps*. Charles Sheldon wrote a beautiful account of what happened when the members of one church began to ask the question, "What would Jesus do?" That simple question, and their attitude of "putting on the mind of Christ" in every situation, changed the whole city! This story (also sold on videotape by The Chapel Ministries) motivates Christians to search the Scriptures and find out what God wills for each situation. As you too take on the mind of Christ, you'll find even your most confusing circumstances changing to follow His carefully planned steps for your life.

6. Write a letter or a poem to Jesus. It's often easier to get our feelings out when we write them down, and it's important to have some kind of written account of what we're feeling during our most difficult times. Write a word picture of what your present maze feels like—the darkness, loneliness, crazy-mixed-up emptiness. Make it into a metaphor: "I'm lost

in a hole. No one's in here, and it's totally dark..." Be as extensive as you can; get specific in your writing. Then present that poem, letter, or story to the Lord as an offering. Ask Him to show you where He fits into the picture and search for ways He might be able to identify with your feelings.

Especially for Families

7. Make analogies for your kids. When three-year-old Todd comes screaming because big brother Chad hit him, remind your two little ones about Jesus in Pilate's court. Tell Todd about how Christ was beaten and tell Chad how much the people made fun of Jesus, yet He didn't do anything to retaliate. Watch for other opportunities in which you might be able to tell them stories about Jesus (the unfruitful fig tree when they complain that they're hungry, for example). Help them to think along the lines of, "How would Jesus feel, and what would He do?" whenever they run into conflict or difficult conditions.

8. Watch a Jesus video as a family. *The Touch of Jesus* and *Jesus of Nazareth* are popular films that tell the story of Jesus. Actually seeing what might have

happened can help us enter into the emotions of the words we've read over and over again. Go see a Passion play if you have the opportunity, or plan a family movie night around the VCR, complete with popcorn. Afterward, discuss the character of Jesus—what part really touched you? What could you identify with the most, and how might that help you when you don't know what to do? Let this be a time of discovery for the children—help them pick up more of a realization that Jesus was an actual person who can identify with what they feel every day.

Chapter 8

God Plans Surprises

There is a surprise ending to the film *The Madness of King George*, a historic study nominated for four Academy Awards. This screenplay includes a look at the treatment physicians afforded a strange mental affliction that the English monarch suffered. The events take place about a decade after America won her independence.

In one emotional scene, the upset and odd-acting king is, of all places, on the roof of Windsor Castle. The wind is blowing and a full moon shines on an array of chimneys that appear to be a group of observers to this bizarre incident. A concerned and anxious Queen Charlotte, played by Helen Mirien, asks, "Do you think that you are mad?"

King George (Nigel Hawthorne) responds, only making partial sense: "I don't know. I don't know. Madness isn't such a torment. Madness is not half blind. Madness can stand. They skip! They dance! And I talk. I talk and talk and talk. I hear the words, so I have to speak them. I have to empty my head of the words. *Something* has happened. *Something* is not right. Oh, Charlotte." Then the two embrace, weeping in each other's arms.

The field of medicine in the late 1780's was certainly not what it is today. Watching as various treatments are tried on the king, viewers have to wonder how he survived. But he does, and in time George miraculously assumes his royal duties once again. However, his recovery has hardly been due to the skill of his doctors!

At the end of the film a helpful message appears on the screen just before the credits. It reads:

> "The colour of the king's urine suggests he was suffering from porphyria, a physical illness that affects the nervous system. The disease is periodic, unpredictable—and hereditary."

So this was a sickness that comes and goes. It was just a matter of time before the king's symptoms disappeared as though his system had healed itself!

Another film is taking us by surprise, though not because we didn't know how the age-old story ends. Instead, it's the fact that more than 700 million people around the world have seen this historic classic. That's a huge number to watch one movie—700 million!

A new book by Paul Eshleman, the director of this worldwide film project, tells what happened when this feature was shown over Iraqi national television, at the Soviet concert hall in Stalin's birthplace, to resistant Nigerian Muslims in Africa, near the "Killing Fields" of Cambodia, and in Shining Path guerilla territory inside Peru. I have interviewed Paul on both radio and television, and many of the stories he shares fall into the near-miracle category.

This biographical movie has been watched by huge crowds numbering in the tens of thousands. It's also been shown to remote Asian villages where a sheet served as a screen. But here's what's remarkable. A man's life, which to us is almost too well known, quickly brings tears to audiences when the main character is put to death. Then, before long, there is an explosion of applause when he comes alive again. It's like the viewers know this is an account that has to be true. Something inside each one affirms, "Here's the person I have been looking for all my life." This self-authenticating of the Holy Spirit is what makes so many people want to give their lives to this man whose life is chronicled in *The Touch of Jesus.*

I don't believe it's too much to write that the *Jesus* film project has become one of the most remarkable evangelistic tools in recent history. Dr. Bill Bright first thought of producing a film that would closely follow the Gospel accounts of Christ's life. Since being made, it's been shown in 216 countries and translated into more than 320 languages! The Lord is obviously putting His blessing on this outreach in a way that boggles the mind.

Much of the world's population still lives in storytelling cultures, and this movie tells the most powerful story of all. How amazing to think that Christ's role in history, which we know so well, is foreign to so many. But people who aren't acquainted with what happened when Jesus came to earth find that through this film, they are immediately captured by the marvelous love of God's Son. Then the surprise ending almost overwhelms them.

Christ says in John 16:20-22:

...You will grieve, but your grief will turn to joy. A woman giving birth to

a child has pain because her time has come; but when her baby is born she forgets the anguish because of her joy that a child is born into the world. So with you: Now is your time of grief, but I will see you again and you will rejoice, and no one will take away your joy.

Here is history's most amazing turn-about: The worst of defeats becomes the greatest of victories. The angels at the empty tomb summed it up well when they asked the dedicated women who came to anoint Christ's body, "Why do you look for the living among the dead?" (Lk. 24:5)

This ending is not historic irony that by some quirk resolves itself as in *The Madness of King George*. Here is a divine narrative put together before the creation of the world. God is the One responsible for how things turned out, and what He did needs to be told to all. When the magnitude of the Incarnation is grasped, it has a profound effect on lives. That, of course, is exactly what our Lord intended.

I am choosing to live my life with the firm conviction that one of God's outstanding characteristics is that He is full of resurrection-type surprises. One of His specialties is taking an impossible set of circumstances and coming up with new possibilities. When things look so bad that we are tempted to give up, like the early disciples did after the crucifixion, we need to put our hope in the Lord's ability to create amazing turnabouts. He still orchestrates them in ways that rival the accounts we read about in Scripture.

So here's another specific answer to the question of what do when you don't know what to do: *Bad times become good times when you place your hope in the God of surprising outcomes.* I'm believing that this recent tough chapter in my life will soon take a wonderful turn. It's not like God to waste major experiences without putting His special twist on how things end.

Throughout this book I have repeatedly mentioned India. What a perplexing maze that country went through before their independence was finally declared. The history is carefully told in the film *Gandhi*, in which director Richard Attenborough chronicles the life of the deceased Indian leader. Ben Kingsley plays the role of the man Indians called the "Great Soul." I admire Gandhi's tenacity, his "death fasts," and his great concern for his people. How sad that an assassin's bullet cut him down in January of 1948 before he could see the realization of his life's work.

In the 1950's, India began to close its doors to Western missionaries. These servants of the Lord were unfairly seen as a part of the past period of colonialism. To Western Christian leaders, it seemed like a mortal blow to the future of the Church in India. How would the people of that vast subcontinent ever know the message of One far greater and more loving than Gandhi? It's true that Christians could still get passports into India as physicians, educators, and so on. But "tent maker" missionaries could not participate in the type of aggressive evangelism and church planting that would be required.

Although the cause of Christ in India seemed to have come to a standstill, nothing could have been further from the truth. In a most amazing fashion, the Lord began to call out national workers. Dark-skinned men and women began leading the Church, just as Gandhi had in the earlier political setting. Before long a disciplined band of men and women with hot hearts for evangelism and church planting were doing a work few Western missionaries could have imagined.

What happened was actually an advantage to the Kingdom worldwide. A native missionary could live on as little as $30 a month. If in certain settings that was doubled or tripled, it was nothing compared to the cost of Western missionaries. Besides, Christian workers from places like the United States couldn't get into India, even if the extra money was raised.

These new national workers mixed easily with the people they were burdened to reach. They were dedicated, more than adequately educated, and excited about serving Christ. Before long they began to see phenomenal growth mark the Church. Goals were established that were far and above anything Western missionaries would have dreamed. Today when I talk to native missionaries in India, they say almost universally that it is spiritual harvest time in their land. Harvest time—who would have thought it? Praise the Lord.

The largest number of unreached people groups in the world still live in India. But the door is wide open for native missionaries to do evangelism and church planting in these settings. I believe the job will get done because the best and most qualified workers are being challenged to take the hardest assignments—which is probably the way it always should have been.

All this is like divine irony to me. Again, it's God taking what many saw as bad news and making that the springboard for the surprisingly good news He had in mind all along! I believe something truly wonderful will unfold for Christians in all lands where people place their hope in Him as a God of surprising outcomes.

Are you still in the middle of a maze?

I am too. Remember?

I have attempted to be open about my life as I shared my advice about what to do when you don't know what to do. But I have to admit that while writing this final chapter, I was awakened in the middle of the night with a panic attack. Sitting up in bed, all I could think was, "We're not going to make it. This whole thing is going to come crashing down around my head. The surprise is that there won't be a surprise!"

When my wife asked if I was all right, I felt a little like King George responding to Charlotte. "I don't know. *Something* has happened. *Something* is not right. Oh, Karen."

I went downstairs and prayed, but my faith was weak. In my mind the difficulties I faced loomed bigger than what I was able to ask of God. Finally I went back up to bed. Karen's embrace seemed more real to me at the time than the Lord's did.

When Life Becomes a Maze—did you expect a book by an expert? Here's what to do: number one, number two, and so on?

Well, I have tried to be specific in my suggestions because it's what I felt would be most helpful. But I'm not just researching a subject. This isn't a compilation of thoughts from friends who might have a suggestion or two to contribute. Read what I'm saying as lessons learned by a man who understands something of what you're experiencing. I too am still in the middle of the maze, and sometimes I panic about ever making my way out. But I'm not in the maze by myself. The advice I give has been picked up while walking with Another who faced a lot more than any of us will ever begin to know. My traveling companion is Jesus. For me, this year has been one of Christ's repeating, "David, you lost your way, but you didn't lose Me. Take heart...

- "I'll make a path for you through this confusion. Concentrate on My help and not on your problems.
- "Embrace one of My promises. Choose to believe it, or not. There are lots of them—the supply won't run out. They're found all through the Word.
- "Keep your support relationships with other believers strong. That's why I provided My Church for you.

- "Write down the joys that refresh your spirit. My Father will never leave you without daily evidences of His loving care.
- "Get rid of all the clutter you can from your life. You'll find it a lot easier to keep your eyes on Me.
- "You're never going to negotiate a maze without making some mistakes. So remember, these are times to lean heavily on God's grace and forgiveness.
- "Discover how I identify with your struggles. Then let Me be the One to talk you through what needs to be done.
- "Do you recall what one of your Lord's specialties is, David? Good! Then place your hope in Me as the God of surprising outcomes."

That's my current experience. Now friend, maybe it's been a bad year for you like it's been for me. I'm sorry about that. But just because you're lost doesn't mean you've lost Christ. If you stay close to Him, He will help you master your maze.

I'm confident that there's a lot you already know about Jesus. But do this, will you? Picture yourself observing a crowd of people watching the movie, *The Touch of*

Jesus. Maybe it's in Kathmandau, Nepal. Paul Eshleman writes about being there with "Daniel," the native director of the *Jesus* film ministry for that Himalayan country at the "roof of the world." Daniel's commitment to Christ had resulted in his spending two months in jail.

"These prisons were terrible hell-holes, with dirt floors and a bucket at the end of the cell for sanitation. As the government troops heard of people being baptized, they picked them up in groups and threw them into prison. The Christian brothers and sisters brought food and blankets to help them survive their year there. They counted it a privilege to suffer for their Lord.

" 'We ask all Christians to tithe their time,' Daniel explained. 'That means we ask them to give thirty-six days a year to go to other areas to share Christ and show the "JESUS" film.' "

Now, in your imagination you're at one of those Nepalese showings. It's not like watching a film at a church in our land. To show *The Touch of Jesus* in Nepal involves a certain amount of risk on someone's part.

Though the movie is not in your language, you know the story well enough to follow what's happening. But even more than that, you notice the response of the viewers to what they see. You sense their delight in Christ's words, and in His miracles and His love for people. Well into the evening the crowd grows quiet as the scenes begin that lead to the crucifixion. You detect tears and hear sobs. Then you catch their wonderment as the truth of the resurrection begins to impact them. The applause begins again, and the power of this story of the greatest of all people who ever lived encompasses you afresh.

As you sit in silence attempting to process what's taken place, think in your mind that the Jesus of this film comes and sits next to you. He says what I said earlier, "So, My friend, it's been a bad year. I'm sorry about that. But in this setting I thought you might see Me through fresh eyes and hear me through new ears." Then He continues...

- "These people don't know Me as well as you do, but already they believe in Me. Can you trust Me to make a path for you through this confusion? I want you to be an 'I believe' person.
- "Find a promise in Scripture you would like to see God keep. Decide whether you'll believe it or not.

Then dare to embrace it and make it your own.

- "Don't pull away from others. Work at support relationships that will strengthen you. This is important. You need Me, but you need other Christians also.

- "Don't miss the joys My Father goes out of His way to grace you life with. He wants to refresh your spirit.

- "Clutter is not a friend when you're in a situation that's already confusing. Get rid of as much of it as you can.

- "My Father shows special consideration to those in the midst of hard times. Learn to draw on His grace and forgiveness.

- "I know firsthand what you're going through. Believe Me, I can identify with your struggles, and I'd be happy to talk you through a solution I know will work.

- "Never give up hope. Surprising outcomes is one of My Father's specialties. He demonstrated this in My case, and I'm confident He will in yours as well. Tell Him what you would like to have happen. Go over your request to see if it's in line with His best interests as well as yours.

Then say, 'Father, You should also feel free to come up with even a better solution, for I understand You're good at that!' "

Christ—what a marvelous person to teach you what to do when you don't know what to do. I picture Him as an incredibly confident individual because He knew who His Father was. I want to live that way as well. I know the many tragedies that can take place in our world. But if I am God's man walking in obedience to what I believe He wants me to do, I should be confident that the ultimate outcome of my life will be good.

I believe what you and I experience can be like the experiences of the characters in Scripture who serve as examples for us: Joseph, Esther, David, Mary, Moses, and Ruth. Not all their days were filled with sunshine. They knew extreme difficulties. But the Lord exalted them like He did His Son. Why would He want us to know about these men and women if their lessons of faith can't be proved in my life and your life as well?

I'm convinced that the Christian experience was not meant to be lived in a perpetual maze. To desire to get out of confusing situations is a sign of health. You should want a tough time to reverse itself and become a good time. Sometimes that happens spontaneously, as in the case of King George and his doctors. But don't count on it.

If I were you, I'd put my confidence in the way of the other King. I'd follow His prescriptions, assuming that down through the centuries His practice has more than proven itself. I'd take to heart what He has to say. The touch of Jesus, that's what I recommend.

What to Do

Here are some suggestions to help you live out what you've learned in this chapter.

1. Don't complain until the end of the day. If you get stuck in traffic and are half an hour late for a sales meeting, don't grumble all the way there. If you spill your breakfast on your sweater and have to wear a dress because everything else is in the laundry, don't bother to get upset. You may find that your meeting was postponed an hour, or you might bump into someone you wanted to impress—who happens to love that dress! God has a way of working things out in surprising ways, but we take all the joy out of those surprises when we complain before waiting to see what He will do.

2. Tell "happily ever after" stories. Invite an "old saint"—someone who's been a Christian for a long time—over for dinner and conversation. Invite him or her to tell you about the times in life when things appeared terribly confusing and hard, but had a happy ending. You may hear about some crazy little incidents ("Would you believe I once drove the wrong car home from the shopping mall

and the owner sent the police after me?") as well as some heartwarming description of God's somehow bringing His child through an incredible maze. Whatever the stories, everyone around your table will have a chance to laugh over a meal together as people share how God has taken care of them in the most surprising ways.

3. Plan your garden. Sit down with some seed catalogs and explore God's wonderful plant creations. Pick out something you'd like to plant and, if you can afford it, order it. When the seed or the bulb comes, examine it carefully. It doesn't look much like the picture in your garden catalog, does it? Hold on to the hope that when it's planted the dead seed will resurrect as a flower, a constant evidence of how God can make even your hardest, ugliest situations beautiful.

4. Look into literature. Many classic books, plays, and biographies have surprising redemptive conclusions; consider Charles Dickens's *Tale of Two Cities*, William Shakespeare's *Winter's Tale*, and Alexander Solzhenitsen's *Oak and the Calf*. Read one of these and think about how God is much bigger than the "fate" to which your book may

have attributed its outcome. Or reflect on how the same God you serve actually constructed that exciting ending! Then thank Him for how He can do the same in your situation.

5. Mark up your Bible. Buy an inexpensive Bible (you can find them at discount stores for as little as five dollars), and spend some time highlighting the stories and verses that demonstrate God's love of surprising outcomes. You don't have to spend hours upon hours studying. Just take it with you wherever you go and, when you have a few minutes, skim and highlight. You may be able to finish one of Paul's letters during your train commute to work, or you may finish up the Book of Ruth while your husband is driving the family to church. Read quickly, searching out the great things God did back then, remembering that He can do the same today. Then keep that copy of the Bible as a reference for whenever you need encouragement. It'll be easy to find examples of those exciting surprises—just look for the colored words!

Especially for Families

6. Go on a "God hunt." Teach your children to look for the surprises God gives them

throughout the day. Every time you notice that God has done something wonderful, call it a "God-hunt sighting." Ask them at the end of the day whether they saw God working in their lives. What surprises did He bring to them? Encourage their excitement in hunting for those special, unexpected ways God reveals Himself to us.

7. Review the story of the ugly duckling. Hans Christian Anderson's "Ugly Duckling" is a classic that teaches children not to give up hope too quickly. Many teens have clung to that concept during those awkward years when they thought they'd never be a "beautiful swan." But younger kids also can apply the story's principle: God has made us each according to His plan. Just because we don't know how things will turn out doesn't mean He won't surprise us with something wonderful. Read this story as a family and talk about the hope it can bring each of you in your situation.

8. Remember the ant. The next time you see an ant or any tiny bug, bring your kids over to look at it. Let them watch it scramble around for a while, and explain to them that this little insect can't

see what's far ahead. It's pretty busy trying to get down the next few inches of its path—then, who knows what it might encounter? You can tell your children, "The ant might be working as hard as it can to get to the top of a huge hill (which to us doesn't look like much). It might wonder whether all its effort is worth it. But at the top, it might find a huge crumb of chocolate cake! That would be worthwhile, wouldn't it?" Let them know that life is like that sometimes—we struggle through hard times and wonder whether life is worth so much work. But then God comes along with a wonderful surprise, and that makes everything all right.